"Read everything that is good for the good of your soul. Then learn to read as a writer, to search out that hidden machinery, which it is the business of art to conceal and the business of the apprentice to comprehend."

In *The Hidden Machinery*, critically acclaimed and *New York Times* best-selling author Margot Livesey offers a masterclass for those who love reading literature and for those who aspire to write it. Through close readings, arguments about craft, and personal essay, Livesey delves into the inner workings of fiction and considers how our stories and novels benefit from paying close attention both to great works of literature and to our own individual experiences. Her essays range in subject matter from navigating the shoals of research to creating characters that walk off the page, from how Flaubert came to write his first novel to how Jane Austen subverted romance in her last one. As much at home on your nightstand as it is in the classroom *The Hidden Machinery* will become a book readers and writers return to over and over again.

The HIDDEN MACHINERY

Essays on Writing

Published by Tin House Books, Portland, Oregon,
and Brooklyn, New York

Distributed by W. W. Norton & Company

Library of Congress Cataloging-in-Publication Data

Names: Livesey, Margot.
Title: The hidden machinery / by Margot Livesey.
Description: First U.S. edition. | Portland, OR :
    Tin House Books, 2017.
Identifiers: LCCN 2016056392 | ISBN 9781941040683
    (alk. paper)
Subjects: LCSH: Fiction—Authorship. | Creative writing. |
    Livesey, Margot—Authorship.
Classification: LCC PN3355 .L557 2017 | DDC 808.3—dc23
LC record available at https://lccn.loc.gov/2016056392

First US Edition 2017
Printed in the USA
Interior design by Jakob Vala

www.tinhouse.com

The HIDDEN MACHINERY

MACHINERY

Essays on Writing

MARGOT LIVESEY

 TIN HOUSE BOOKS / Portland, Oregon & Brooklyn, New York

CONTENTS

THE HIDDEN MACHINERY

Writing the Life, Shaping the Novel

Life is Monstrous, infinite, illogical, abrupt and poignant; a work of art, in comparison, is neat, finite, self-contained, rational, flowing and emasculate . . . To 'compete with life,' whose sun we cannot look upon, whose passions and diseases waste and slay us, to compete with the flavor of wine, the beauty of the dawn, the scorching of fire, the bitterness of death and separation . . . here are indeed labours for a Hercules in a dress coat, armed with a pen and a dictionary . . . No art is true in this sense; none can 'compete with life' . . .

—ROBERT LOUIS STEVENSON,
"A Humble Remonstrance"

I

ON THE BOOKSHELVES of my house in London are the books I read as a child: Robert Louis Stevenson's *Kidnapped*, Kenneth Grahame's *The Wind in the Willows*, Lewis Carroll's *Alice's Adventures in Wonderland*, George MacDonald's *The Princess and Curdie*, and a strange book called *The Pheasant Shoots Back* by Dacre Balsdon. This last, a kind of *Animal Farm* for birds, describes how a family of pheasants outwits the hunters and lives to fly another season. My great-aunt Jean thought it a suitable gift for my fifth birthday. Certainly I appreciated the sky-blue cover and the simple line drawings, but the black marks that covered the pages were a mystery, and not one I was eager to solve. Reading struck me as much less important than tree climbing or bridge building or visiting the nearby pigs. Sometime that autumn, however, my priorities shifted. I remember standing in the corner of the nursery, where we had our lessons, refusing to read, when, quite suddenly, the words turned from a wall—like the one I was staring at—into a window. I was looking through them at a farmyard filled with animals. I emerged from the corner and read *Percy the Bad Chick.* Here was someone like myself—small, naughty, friendless—yet look how Percy triumphed over the other animals, including Dobbin, the farmer's horse. From then on I embraced books. I had, although the word remained unknown to me for several years, discovered novels.

Who do you want to be when you grow up? the grown-ups around me asked.

Not you, I wanted to say, but I was a well-brought-up child. A nun, I responded, a vet, an explorer, Marie Curie. Each profession came from a book I had read. I was slow to grasp that the person I wanted to be was not someone *between* the covers but behind them. By the time I went to university I had relinquished my ambition to discover a new element and was studying literature and philosophy, mostly the former. Our curriculum began with *Sir Gawain and the Green Knight* and Chaucer and zigzagged erratically forward until we reached Virginia Woolf, still at that time a relatively minor figure. Then we came to an abrupt halt. One faculty member was rumored to be doing research into a living author, the Australian novelist Patrick White, but that was a private activity; he lectured on the safely interred: Eliot, Pound, and Joyce. Nonetheless news reached me from the larger world that there were authors—Saul Bellow, Margaret Drabble, Doris Lessing, Solzhenitsyn—living, breathing, making novels out of the fabric of contemporary life. Among my fellow students one or two claimed to be writing poetry, but the evidence was scanty.

The year after I graduated from university I went traveling in Europe and North Africa with my boyfriend of the time. He was writing a book on the philosophy of science and after a few weeks, bored with exploring cathedrals and markets alone, I began to write a book too. I did not know enough to write a history of the Crusades, or a biography of the Brontës, but, after sixteen years of reading, I felt amply qualified to write a novel. After all, this was the only training that most of my favorite writers had undergone. "Read good authors with passionate attention," runs Robert Louis Stevenson's advice to a young writer, "refrain altogether from reading bad ones."

I began writing "The Oubliette" in October. (The title refers, with unwitting irony, to the French dungeon in which prisoners were kept until they were forgotten.) In campsites and cheap hotels I did my best to imitate Trollope, writing for so many hours a day. I wrote in pencil, rubbing out frequently, on every other line of a spiral notebook. I filled one notebook, began another, and filled that too. My novel was growing. By the following June I had a draft: four hundred pages of made-up people, doing made-up things. While I wrote, I was doing my best to follow Stevenson's advice. I read Richard Brautigan and Elizabeth Bowen, Malcolm Lowry and Edna O'Brien, Henry James and Ralph Ellison, *The Tale of Genji*, and lots of Russians. It was a year of glorious reading. Then, shortly before my twenty-second birthday, in a campsite in Romania, I sat down to read something less than glorious.

Ever since I read *Percy the Bad Chick*, books had transported me. When I opened *Great Expectations*, sentences and paragraphs vanished. I was on the marsh with Pip and the fearsome convict. But "The Oubliette" left me obstinately earthbound. Once again I was staring at a wall, rather than through a window. I told myself that this strange stodginess was the burden of authorship: words, which could transport others, were mute to their maker.

One respect in which I followed Stevenson's advice during my year of travel was by reading two of the many authors who had been excluded from my university curriculum: Henry James and E. M. Forster. I bought *The Portrait of a Lady* before we left England.

As for Forster, he was enjoying a wave of popularity. In hostels and bookshops there was almost invariably a secondhand copy of *Howards End* or *A Room with a View*. These novels were the opposite of mute; they resonated with my Scottish childhood full of tacit agreements and dark betrayals. How well James and Forster understood that embarrassment is a major emotion, that we are all governed by the opinions of others and by the great triumvirate of class, money, and, in Forster's case, race. Of course I believed myself, as I wandered the gardens of the Alhambra, or explored the Casbah of Tangiers, to be a successful fugitive from such bourgeois notions. What a pleasure it was to look back on that world I had left behind. "Only connect," I murmured.

Forster's work, in particular, enchanted me, but what did his witty, urbane novels have to do with mine? Unfortunately, not much. I had no idea, not an inkling, of how he put together his seamless, deeply serious books. The notion of dismantling a novel, of examining, say, the point of view or the transitions, was still entirely foreign. But even if I had attempted to take apart a few chapters of *Howards End*, I suspect I would have been baffled. Forster is so tenacious in his intelligence, so deft in his handling of point of view, so subtle in his structure. And then there is the voice, the penetrating, insightful voice, rising over everything, controlling every umbrella and slipper and semicolon.

It took me several years to understand that "The Oubliette" was bad in more ways than I can easily enumerate. It was simultaneously farfetched and boring; the characters spoke like Nazis in old British films, their English oddly stiff; the descriptions read as if they came from guidebooks, which, in some cases, they had. I had no sense of pacing; no thought for what sort of unit a chapter could, or should, be; no understanding of the importance of setting; and, perhaps strangest of all, no notion of the crucial role of suspense, especially in longer fiction. James describes his heroine Isabel Archer as riding in a coach. As a reader, I had spent many happy hours riding in various coaches, reaching many marvelous destinations, but I knew almost nothing about how they were built, what made the wheels turn. I had entirely failed to be influenced by my years of ardent reading.

How was this possible? Harold Bloom's phrase "the anxiety of influence" has so thoroughly entered our culture that it is easy to underestimate how hard it is to be influenced, really influenced, by another artist. If only I could read *Middlemarch* and write a novel half as good. When I looked up "influence" in the Oxford English Dictionary, I was surprised to discover that the first meaning is "[t]he action of flowing in, influx"; the second "[a] supposed emanation of ethereal fluid or occult force from the stars." Our most common meaning comes fourth: "[a]n action exerted, imperceptibly or by indirect means, by one person or thing on another so as to cause changes in conduct, development, conditions, etc." I like how this definition emphasizes the stealthy nature of influence—something that transforms us when we're not paying attention—but for the practicing artist influence requires a more active engagement. We must work to be influenced, not merely wait.

Even worse than all the problems with "The Oubliette" that I have already mentioned was my failure to understand that irrelevance is a fatal sin. One thing I knew about novels was that they went on for a while, so I dutifully threw in a mass of detail. I described the toast, the trees, the birds, the curtains. This, I thought, was what the project of realism was all about. Putting aside that misunderstanding, how could I have comprehended the deeply complicated question of relevance when, after months of work, I could not explain what truly interested me in the material. (I am echoing here W. H. Auden's dazzlingly simple advice to a young poet: write about what most interests you.) I wanted to write a novel, not necessarily this one.

My experience, I've learned over several decades of engaging with young writers, was not unusual. Because we come to reading and writing so early—as a life skill, not an art form—people often overestimate their own abilities as fiction writers. "Oh, yes, I'm thinking of writing a novel," my fellow passengers tell me on planes and trains. As soon as we consider Serena Williams playing tennis, or Yo-Yo Ma playing the cello, we recognize the absurdity of thinking that one can easily move from audience member to performer. No one would imagine that all they had to do was listen to music and then they'd be able to play at Carnegie Hall, or watch Wimbledon and then enter the Davis Cup.

I did revise "The Oubliette" to the best of my ability and I did find an agent for it. He sent it around, and various editors sent it back. I learned to dread the words "quiet," "beautiful," "promising." Meanwhile I had begun to write stories. I still didn't realize how much I had to learn as a writer, but I knew that I did not want to keep making mistakes over several hundred pages. Besides, my year of travel was over and stories fit better with the split shifts I was working as a waitress in Toronto. I wrote in the morning before going to serve lunch to harried office workers and again in the afternoon before the more enviable dinner crowd showed up. I kept reading omnivorously, but I was still a long way from doing what the novelist Francine Prose recommends in *Reading Like a Writer* (and an even longer way from thinking of myself as a writer). Although I was distressed by my failure to be influenced, I was, like many young artists, more concerned with originality than with craft. I wrote a story called "A History of Defenestration" about a series of people being thrown out of windows and another—I briefly had a job cleaning an art gallery—called "A Story to Be Illustrated by Max Ernst."

A turning point in my snail's progress came when the Irish novelist Brian Moore spent a term at the University of Toronto as writer in residence. The secretary who made his appointments did not question my credentials, and I turned up in my waitress's black skirt and white blouse, nervously clutching a story. What Mr. Moore did next was astonishing. From the breast pocket of his tweed jacket, he produced a fountain pen. Then he read the story aloud, imitating all the characters and the animals; the story was set in the Scottish countryside of my childhood.

"Now would she say that?" he pondered. "Or should there be a little more about the ponies, that nickering sound they make?" He would jot a note in the margin.

I would go home and throw myself back into the story, guided by his neatly written comments. I brought him "The Salt Course" six weeks in a row, and each time he read it aloud. No detail was too small for his attention. He showed me that the actual words—which, since my struggles with *Percy*, I had ceased to apprehend individually—could make all the difference. He showed me that a good sentence speaks even to its maker and that we often recognize our own mediocrity, even when we pretend not to. Now, after years of teaching, I admire both his kindness and his acumen in not allowing me to leave a single sheet of paper on his desk.

So I asked people how they wanted their steak done and whether they cared for dessert, and I continued to write. At the age of thirty I knew no one else who wrote fiction, or even aspired to, but the stories crept into print. I published a collection and moved, in one of those odd swerves that American life permits, from waitressing to teaching. One day I read a letter in a British newspaper written by a woman seeking advice about her daughter. Nine-year-old Louise dominated the family with her fierce temper and fanatical sense of order. She complained if a chair was moved an inch, if her father arrived home five minutes late. Holidays were out of the question. Her brothers, both older, were afraid to cross her, and neither punishment nor reward reached her. I still recall the heartbreaking ending of the letter as the writer watched her husband prepare to leave her, her sons grow increasingly aloof. "If my spouse behaved like this," she wrote, "I could divorce him, but how can I divorce my daughter?"

This letter resonated with me on a number of levels. As a well-behaved child, I had watched my father honor my stepmother's every whim. Then, in my early twenties, I had myself become an absentminded stepmother, struggling with the other side of the equation. So I was keenly interested in what occurs when romantic and familial love collide. Over the course of several months I tried to fit my version of Louise into twenty pages, twenty-five maximum. Eventually, reluctantly, I was forced to accept that the psychological arc of the narrative—the changes and transformations—required the space of a novel.

Most of my students were working on short stories. I was reading them, I was teaching them, I was suggesting strategies for revising them. Perhaps no surprise that one of the first editorial comments on *Homework* was that I had written a story writer's novel. Every chapter ended with a revelation or a denouement. Close the book, dear reader, I might as well have said. My years of working on short fiction had taught me much about character, scene, and sentence but little about that eloquent balancing of long and short lines of suspense that the novel requires. Despite my desire to be influenced, and many happy hours of reading, I had not yet figured out the hidden machinery in the novels I loved.

II

Adela Quested arrived in bookshops forty-six years after Isabel Archer, and the two are opposites in almost every way; it is only fitting that they inhabit such opposite novels. How firmly James gives his instructions to the reader in his title and in his opening description of three men—Mr. Touchett; his son, Ralph; and their friend, Lord Warburton—having afternoon tea on the lawn of an English country house, waiting for the arrival of a young American woman. Onto that gilded lawn steps Isabel Archer, whom James tells us only one man in twenty will have the discrimination to appreciate and with whom everyone, save her husband, falls in love. James too is in love with Isabel—he shares her opinion that she is, in some indefinable way, extraordinary—and everything in the novel is designed to reveal that extraordinariness. He never stops to ask why we are paying so much attention to a young woman with no obvious talents or significant accomplishments; nor do we.

Adela Quested too is arriving, in India, after a long voyage, but there is no red carpet for her. No one, not even her fiancé, Ronny, is waiting urgently for her arrival. Poor Adela. From the moment she is introduced in chapter three of *A Passage to India* as "the queer, cautious girl," she is subjected to Forster's harshest scrutiny: she is plain; she is confused; her aspirations to goodness, to understand India, to avoid the thoughtless racism of her compatriots, only lead to muddle, and worse. And in the many negative comments on her appearance we sense Forster's complicated feelings about women. Aziz is outraged at being accused of molesting Adela not least because she is ugly.

Although there are many differences in the form and content of these two novels, the kinship between their authors is clear. James is Forster's most immediate ancestor with respect to his gift for psychological insight and his deliberate use of travel. His Americans come to Europe. Forster's English men and women go to Italy, or India. Both are sharply aware of the fictional possibilities of leaving home and of how new landscapes can reveal issues of culture and class, as well as the spiritual lives of their protagonists. Each deals with sex in a shadowy, veiled fashion.

James's machinery seems, at first glance, more straightforward than Forster's, as does his journey to writing the novel. In 1876, the year after he published *Roderick Hudson*, he moved to London. The years immediately following find him referring, in both notebooks and letters, to his new, big novel. When his brother, William James, pronounced *The Europeans* thin, Henry wrote back, "I don't at all despair, yet, of doing something fat." In a letter to his mother he described the new novel as being to his previous work like wine to water. But first he had to create some breathing space. He cashed in on the success of *Daisy Miller* by the rapid writing and publication of three shorter works: *The Europeans, Washington Square,* and *Confidence.* This productivity put him in a position to negotiate what, for most writers, would be the opposite of breathing space. He arranged simultaneous serialization of an unwritten novel in the *Atlantic* in America and *MacMillan's* in Britain, originally promising between six and eight monthly episodes and finally producing fourteen. He began work in the spring of 1880; the first episode was published that autumn.

From his title, *The Portrait of a Lady,* onward, James never loses sight of the large questions: What will Isabel Archer do? What will become of her? This is the long line of suspense that governs the novel from first to last. And within the scope of that long line, he poses many smaller questions, which, like the arches of a viaduct, carry us from chapter to chapter: Who is Mrs. Touchett's friend Madame Merle? Will Henrietta

Stackpole alienate everyone? Will Gilbert Osmond's daughter, Pansy, be allowed to marry her heart's desire? Will Isabel ever discover that Ralph is responsible for her inheritance? Will Caspar Goodwood, her stalwart American suitor, ever give up? As one question is answered, another opens up, leading us onward, ever onward.

James was vitally aware of the need to earn what he calls "the writer's living wage": the reader's attention. In the preface to the revised edition of *Portrait*, written with nearly thirty years of hindsight, he muses on the danger of having too little story and claims to have taken every possible provision for the reader's amusement. But this was not how the opening chapters struck W. D. Howells, his editor at the *Atlantic*. After the first couple of episodes Howells wrote to complain that Isabel was overanalyzed and that there was too much of Henrietta. James's sister, Alice, following in the family tradition of vigorous criticism, went further and pondered whether Isabel would ever befriend someone like Henrietta. James agreed with Howells and defended himself against Alice. In the preface he remarks, "It is a familiar truth to the novelist, at the strenuous hour, that, as certain elements in any work are of the essence, so others are only of the form." Some characters, he continues, belong to the subject directly; others but indirectly. Henrietta is an example of the latter. James compares her first to one of the wheels of the coach where "the subject alone is ensconced, in the form of its 'hero and heroine.'" Then, shifting the metaphor slightly, he comments that Henrietta may run beside the coach for all she's worth, may cling to it until she's out of breath, but that she never so much as gets her foot on the step. Isabel, James reminds us repeatedly, is a heroine in the Shakespearean sense: for all her greatness she has a fatal flaw. While the coach may dawdle during those early pages—stop too often to change horses or admire the view—once Isabel arrives in Italy and meets Osmond, it hurtles along until that chilling moment in chapter forty-two when, seated beside the dying fire, she finally understands that, through the machinations of Madame Merle and her own vanity, she has been lured into marrying a man who does not love her, who indeed hates her.

James wrote the novel with enviable fluency, much of it while living in hotels in Italy. Those early chapters in which he fusses over Isabel, explaining and reexplaining her, pay off in the later ones as he drives forward to what interests him, ignoring all else. He does not show us Osmond proposing to Isabel, for instance, or their wedding. And it is here that we can see how he is taking the biographical novel to new heights, and new depths.

His handling of time signals that he has left behind the tradition of *Moll Flanders* and *David Copperfield*. We learn little about Isabel's childhood, nothing about what follows her last conversation with Caspar Goodwood. James's focus is entirely on her spiritual journey. In a review of *Middlemarch* written ten years earlier, he described Dorothea as a young woman destined for a larger moral life. The same might be said of Isabel and, like Dorothea, she mistakes her means of achieving that largeness. Gilbert Osmond is her Casaubon.

James's structure, the heroine in the coach, is a familiar one, and he embraces it with full consciousness. One of the things he criticizes in *Middlemarch* is the way the novel alternates between the two main characters. Even while he admires Lydgate as one of the best portraits of a man penned by a woman, he complains that George Eliot is not focusing sufficiently on Dorothea; he wants her to be in the coach all the time. Moreover, he complains that after Casaubon dies, the only remaining question about her is the rather trivial one of whether she will marry Will Ladislaw. He would surely have given *A Passage to India* a similarly mixed review, perhaps echoing the reservations voiced by Lionel Trilling in his famous critique of the novel. "The characters," Trilling writes, "are in the events, the events are not in them: we want a larger Englishman than Fielding, a weightier Indian than Aziz." Forster, he concludes, is writing a political novel of an unusual kind, one in which "the characters are of sufficient size for the plot; they are not large enough for the story—and that indeed is the point of the story."

If I understand him correctly, Trilling is criticizing what others might regard as one of the great virtues of *Passage*: Forster's determination not to have a hero, or a heroine. Adela does something heroic when, at the eleventh hour, in the courtroom, she takes back her accusation of Aziz and in doing so makes herself a pariah in the English community. But she is not allowed to be a heroine. No one is riding in Forster's coach; everyone is clinging to the wheels as it careens along.

This lack of a hero, of an obvious center of empathy, leads to an even more subtle balancing of the long and short lines of suspense, a subtlety that must have been particularly acute for Forster's original readers, many of whom would have known the formulaic Indian romances (an early version of Bollywood) that were popular at that time. I have to confess that on first reading *Passage*, I had no idea what the large question—the long line of suspense—was, but read happily from one small question to the next. Will the bridge party, intended to bring the Indians and the English together, succeed? Will Adela accept Ronny's proposal of marriage? Will Aziz and Fielding become friends? Will Adela recant? When the last veil finally falls, in the triumphant third section, "Temple," and Forster shows his hand at last, I gasped with recognition and delight. Of course, this had been here all along, since the moonlit night when Aziz meets Mrs. Moore in the mosque, but reading as I was in the Jamesian tradition, looking for someone to ride in the coach, I had failed to notice other possibilities.

In early drafts of my novel *Homework* I did have someone riding in the coach, my narrator, and I did have a long line of suspense—would she win the battle with her stepdaughter?—but, as my decisive chapter endings showed, I had no notion of how to manage the shorter lines of suspense, how to persuade both characters and readers to move from one chapter to the next. In other respects, too, *Homework* was the work of a story writer. Although I knew enough to set the novel in a city I loved, Edinburgh, and to give the characters jobs I was familiar with, I did not yet grasp the importance in a novel of what might crudely be called "stuff": the particular circumstances of the characters' lives that render them vivid and credible. In a short story you can get away with a sentence or two about a character's job or house, but in a novel, or at least most novels, it is essential to give the characters occupations as well as preoccupations; perhaps never more so than when the plot is basically domestic. James, even at his best, is short on stuff; Henrietta, a working journalist, represents some gesture toward filling that gap, but he cannot resist letting the other characters make fun of her. He himself cared passionately about earning a living, fussing over contracts and royalties, but his characters are not allowed to. Like Forster, he uses setting, especially houses, as stuff.

Much of my work in revising *Homework* involved learning how to connect the short lines of suspense and how to make better use of the stuff of the novel. I also had to remind myself that my two excellent editors (one in New York, one in Toronto) were not infallible. By this time I was letting Stevenson down on a regular basis, reading many contemporary novels. Publication, I had discovered, was conferred on a number of less-than-perfect books, and all these books, I reminded myself, had editors. Even as I followed my editors' suggestions, I clung to the lesson Brian Moore had taught me: I was still the author and every sentence mattered. A single superfluous phrase, an inappropriate adjective or clumsy adverb, could spoil an otherwise eloquent paragraph. If I was bored while my characters made dinner or made love, then my readers would be too.

III

Along with their sense of character and their gift for using setting to reveal it, James and Forster share another writerly strength: both were keen observers of the world around them and both knew how to transform their observations into art. Over and over in James's notebooks, we see the raw material of his fiction—the gesture, the glance, the secret vanity, the little misstep—captured and brooded upon. Dinner parties, as Leon Edel felicitously remarks, were his laboratory. Forster had the same acute gift for noticing what he needed for his work. The loss of a collar stud on his first visit to India in 1912 became, ten years later, a piercing incident when Aziz lends Fielding his collar stud only to be criticized later for his slovenly dress. Paradoxically one of the many things I needed to learn from reading books was how to read the world. Part of what makes the hidden machinery work is an author's grasp of the telling detail.

Forster's long relationship with India began in 1906 when he was invited to tutor the adopted son of some neighbors who had recently returned from Delhi. At the time he was twenty-seven, stifled by living with his mother in the suburbs, deeply uncertain about almost every aspect of his life. Syed Ross Masood was seventeen, tall, dashing, and confident. Despite, or because of, their differences the two swiftly became friends and remained so after Masood graduated from Oxford and returned to India. When *Howards End* was published in 1910, Forster used his royalties to visit Masood, and other friends, in India. In the course of his travels, meeting Indians both Muslim and Hindu, and various English administrators, Forster became convinced that imperial power inevitably coarsens and corrupts—a view that would be strengthened a few years later by the Amritsar massacre. He began *A Passage to India* after his return to England and managed to write eight chapters before setting the pages aside in favor of *Maurice*, his only openly gay novel. But in the face of the First World War, fiction struck him as increasingly futile. December 31, 1914, finds him announcing in his diary, "Shall never complete another novel." *Maurice*, too, was abandoned.

Forster spent most of the war in Egypt, working for the Red Cross in Alexandria. During those years he produced a slew of pamphlets and critical works but no fiction. Then, in 1921, he returned to India for six months to serve as secretary to His Highness Tukoji Rao III. He hoped a second visit might revive his novel, but he found His Highness's court a muddle and India, in the wake of the massacre, greatly changed. His friend Malcolm Darling had described to him the awful events of that day in 1919 when the English killed or wounded more than a thousand unarmed Indians. An atmosphere of suspicion ruled, and anyone suspected of terrorism could be arrested and held indefinitely without trial. Forster's chapters, rather than coming to life, did the opposite. "As soon as they were confronted with the country they purported to describe," he writes, "they seemed to wilt and go dead and I could do nothing with them."

But back in England, urged on by Leonard Woolf, he returned to those wilted pages. The clear plot of 1913—Adela was assaulted by Aziz in the cave; Aziz was brought to trial—was abandoned, and instead Forster conjured onto the page a masterpiece of obliquity, a dazzling refutation of omniscience. The first chapter of *Passage* is devoted not to any of the characters but to the setting that will govern everything: the Marabar Caves, the city of Chandrapore, the river, and the sky. The second chapter introduces Dr. Aziz, arguing with his friends as to whether it is possible for an Indian to be friends with an Englishman, a question that Forster had been asking himself ever since he met Masood. Later, after being snubbed by his white superior, Aziz stops at the mosque and meets the sympathetic Mrs. Moore. So Forster, just as surely as James, sets his hidden machinery to work. His characters do not share Isabel Archer's illusion of self-determination; they know themselves to be in the grip of larger forces and it is how they respond to these forces, as much as to each other, that determines their fates. Finally, on January 21, 1924, Forster declared the novel finished. With no special effort it was published in early June of that year and became his biggest success, critically and commercially.

Reading *A Passage to India* gives no clue to its tattered history, the fits and starts in which it was composed, the uncertainties that Forster suffered throughout and especially in writing the scenes set in the Marabar Caves. It is illuminating to compare one of the many early drafts of this scene with the final version. In 1913 he wrote: "She [Adela] struck out and he got hold of her other hand and forced her against the wall, he got both her hands in one of his, and then felt at her breasts. 'Mrs. Moore' she yelled. 'Ronny—don't let him, save me.'" Nearly a decade later Forster sets up Adela and Mrs. Moore's visit to the caves with great skill, gradually separating Adela and Aziz from their chaperones; first Fielding and Godbole miss the train (Godbole was praying), and then Mrs. Moore is taken ill. As Adela and Aziz approach a group of caves accompanied only by a guide, Adela, thinking about her forthcoming marriage, asks Aziz whether he is married and then, "in her honest, decent, inquisitive way," how many wives he has. "One, one in my own particular case," sputters Aziz. Dismayed and angry, he plunges into one of the several caves. Adela, "quite unconscious that she had said the wrong thing, and not seeing him," also goes into a cave. There the chapter ends. We never learn what exactly happened to Adela. The author himself, later in life, always claimed not to know.

Forster's decade of gestation was a time not only of widespread political upheaval but also of huge private changes. Living in Alexandria, he became friends with the poet C. P. Cavafy, who, unlike Forster, was openly homosexual. By both precept and example Cavafy encouraged the shy Englishman to new boldness. In October 1916 Forster wrote to his friend Florence Berger, "Yesterday for the first time in my life I parted with respectability." He was thirty-eight years old. Not long after he became deeply involved with a young Egyptian train conductor, Mohammed el Adl.

Inevitably we speculate, with Forster's encouragement, that the falling of that final barrier and his subsequent relations contributed to the rewriting of the cave scene and the stripping away of physical detail. Adela's visit to the caves and her subsequent accusation of Aziz turn out to be the center of the book but not, in some odd way, the climax. The third section of the novel, "Temple," which takes place two years later, shows us that Forster is pursuing something altogether larger, more ineffable, than the fuss about Adela, or even than the burning question of whether an Indian and an Englishman can be friends.

"I ask you," Fielding says to Godbole, "did he [Aziz] do it or not? Is that plain?"

Godbole replies:

> "I am informed that an evil action was performed in the Marabar Hills, and that a highly esteemed English lady is now seriously ill in consequence. My answer to that is this: that action was performed by Dr. Aziz." He stopped and sucked in his thin cheeks. "It was performed by the guide." He stopped again. "It was performed by you." Now he had an air of daring and of coyness. "It was performed by me." He looked shyly down the sleeve of his own coat. "And by my students. It was even performed by the lady herself. When evil occurs, it expresses the whole of the universe. Similarly when good occurs."

Forster, like James, is after the age-old moral questions. When Isabel at last understands the truth about

Madame Merle, she wonders whether she has encountered a phenomenon that she had previously known only from the Bible: wickedness.

IV

As I trust is obvious, I am using the phrase "the hidden machinery" to refer to two different aspects of novel making: on the one hand how certain elements of the text—characters, plot, imagery—work together to make an overarching argument; on the other how the secret psychic life of the author, and the larger events of his or her time and place, shape that argument. This second aspect is one that James would surely have denied and Forster, reluctantly, endorsed. In an essay he published in 1925, "Anonymity: An Inquiry," Forster writes:

> The personality of the writer does become important after we have read his book and begin to study it. When the glamour of creation ceases, when the leaves of the divine tree are silent, when the co-partnership (between writer and reader) is over, then a book changes its nature, and we can ask ourselves questions about it such

as "What is the author's name?" "Where did he live?" "Was he married?" "Which was his favourite flower?" . . . Study is only a serious form of gossip.

When he drafted the opening chapters of *A Passage to India* in 1913, Forster could have pushed forward and written an English-in-India novel, a darker version of *A Room with a View*. He had, after all, written four novels without much trouble. But he needed certain things to happen—a war, a massacre, the discovery of his own sexual nature and of how he too could be corrupted by the white man's power in India—before he knew where the coach was going and who, if anyone, was going to occupy it. Both inner and outer events were required before he could write a novel that simultaneously conveys the monstrous messiness of life and the neatness of art.

James seems to provide a simpler model; he mostly ignores the muddle of world events and his own psyche in favor of the finite rationality of art. Indeed, in *Aspects of the Novel* Forster points to *The Ambassadors* (1903) as a prime example of a novel that relies too heavily on patterning: "Beauty has arrived, but in too tyrannous a guise." *Portrait* remains free of this tyranny, perhaps in part because it draws more freshly on some of James's primary material. His cousin Minny Temple, with her eager curiosity and wide smile, who died at twenty-four, is commonly believed to be the inspiration behind Isabel Archer. But surely his heroine's journey is also fueled in large measure by James's own ambitions; he wants to believe that he too is exceptional, that he too has a larger spiritual life. For him the doorway to that exceptionalness is art; for Isabel it is the doorway her maker can never open: heterosexual marriage.

While the workings of *Portrait* are easier to understand, the skill with which James leads his heroine from one misstep to the next, one insight to the next, is of such delicacy, and such ferocity, that we have to work hard to be influenced. As he wrote of Dorothea, to show a character's soul is no easy matter. Daisy Miller and later Catherine Sloper in *Washington Square* are touching but limited creations when compared to Isabel Archer, with her overweening ambition, her deep intelligence, and her sense that she is destined for extraordinary things.

Stevenson's advice to the young writer is misleadingly simple, a Zen koan in disguise. Read everything that is good, nothing that is bad. And then what? Perhaps if he had written at more length he might helpfully have expanded on his imperatives. Read everything that is good for the good of your soul. Then, learn to read as a writer, to search out that hidden machinery, which it is the business of art to conceal and the business of the apprentice to comprehend. Research, to the degree that it is illuminating, how the author's life informs the text. Read work that is less than good, work in progress, to see that machinery more clearly. Learn to read your own work as if it were that of another. Try to figure out what interests you at the deepest level but do not expose the secret parts of yourself to unkind scrutiny. What are you drawn to? What do you avoid? Admit your own mediocrity and believe in the optimism of revision.

And then, then you have to hope for grace and luck, the Lares and Penates of fiction, to knock at your door. The kind of luck that brought Forster on his second visit to India to the nine-day festival commemorating the birth of Krishna (one of the several incarnations of Vishnu, the preserver), and which he transformed into the gorgeous third section of *A Passage to India* when, at last, he allows Fielding and Aziz to meet and, fleetingly, overcome their misunderstandings. In the more than four decades that followed, Forster wrote nonfiction, criticism, reviews, almost weekly letters to the newspaper about miscarriages of justice, and revised *Maurice,* which was published posthumously, to give the novel a happy ending, but he wrote no new novels. James continued to be prolific for thirty years after Isabel stepped onto the lawn. Both men hid their secrets in their work; each reminds us that few writers get steadily better; many get unsteadily so.

MRS. TURPIN READS THE STARS

Creating Characters Who Walk off the Page

As if they were our own handiwork, we place a high value on our characters.

—**EPICURUS**, "Vatican Sayings,"
third century BC

AS A READER I have no trouble identifying vivid characters. I recognize them the moment they appear on the page. Oh, here she comes, I say, as Becky Sharp hurls a book from the carriage window or Miss Havisham, in her bridal gear, commands Pip and Estella to play cards. Becky and Miss Havisham don't stay on the page; they walk right off it, and take up residence in their readers' imaginations. Vivid characters are not necessarily the sine qua non of memorable fiction, but they are certainly a significant part of it and an enormous part of all fiction. The ordinary reader, E. M. Forster's passenger on the Clapham omnibus (insofar as he or she survives these days), still persists in flying in the face of literary theory and discussing characters in novels and stories as if they were real people. Writers tend to do the same. In a letter to a friend, the Russian novelist Pushkin wrote of one of his characters, "My

Stella has run off and got married. I never would have thought it of her."

So it seems decidedly odd to be deficient in such a major aspect of making fiction—like a golfer who can't putt, or a drummer with no sense of rhythm—but such, I have to confess, is my situation. I am character handicapped. Rereading my early drafts, I discover that I introduce almost every character in terms of eyes (color, shape, glasses/no glasses) and hair (color, length, texture). Of course the range is fairly small, brown or blue, dark or fair, with an occasional Scottish redhead. Then I allow my flimsy beings four gestures:

> they look
> they turn
> they nod
> they shrug

These characters, lacking nearly all necessities of life, remain—not surprisingly—adamantly one-dimensional. They are barely on the page, so how can they leave it?

The more complex and engaging characters that do appear in my later drafts are largely the result of craft and of some measure of that writerly good luck we always need as we approach our work. I used to feel that the effort I put into creating my characters was an embarrassing secret, something to be concealed at all costs. Weren't they a little less vivid, a little less credible, if they hadn't sprung fully formed onto the page? But here's the odd thing. Teaching in graduate programs, and exchanging work with other writers, I've come to realize that I am far from alone in my difficulties. Some authors do have an instinctive feel for character, but many, if not most, have to work hard to people their fictions. To paraphrase Flannery O'Connor's famous remark about story, everyone knows what a character is until she or he sits down to create one.

What does craft consist of? And what makes a reader believe that these little black marks—you are reading them now—in some mysterious way designate a being about whom she can care and argue and have opinions? One of the main obstacles to answering these questions is the way in which successful characters spring to life so quickly, and obscure the artistry by which they're made. Before we examine some lasting characters, let us look at a few of those admirable books of criticism that have accompanied writers over the centuries to see what guidance they offer in this tricky business.

To begin at the beginning: Aristotle's *Poetics*. When I turned back to this seminal work, I was surprised to discover that Aristotle devotes only one of his twenty-six sections to character, and he was almost certainly not using the term in quite the way we do now. He is much more concerned with questions of poetry and plot, comedy and tragedy. In section fifteen, he at last turns to character and offers his usual succinct opinions:

> In respect of character there are four things to be aimed at. First, and most important, it must be good. Now any speech or action that manifests moral purpose of any kind will be expressive of character: the character will be good if the purpose is good. This rule is relative to each class. Even a woman may be good, and also a slave; though the woman may be said to be an inferior being, and the slave quite worthless. The second thing to aim at is propriety. There is a type of manly valor; but valor in a woman, or unscrupulous cleverness, is inappropriate. Thirdly, character must be true to life: for this is a distinct thing from goodness and propriety, as here described. The fourth point is consistency, for though the subject of the imitation, who suggested the type be inconsistent, still he must be consistently inconsistent.

Most of us nowadays would take issue with Aristotle's notions of propriety and repudiate his class system, but much of what he says still makes admirable sense. Although we might think these demands somewhat contradictory—to be good and true to life, to have propriety and be true to life—what emerges is that, for Aristotle, characters in literature are measured against humans and, like humans, are judged by their actions. "All human happiness and misery," he claims, "takes the form of action," an opinion that now echoes through the workshops of America in the form of the oft-repeated, occasionally disputed admonition "Show don't tell." The famously supine Oblomov, hero of the eponymous Russian novel, would have been carried off the stage in act one of any Aristotelian drama; so, I fear, would Bartleby the poor, forlorn scrivener. Aristotle goes on to urge that both plot and character should "aim either at the necessary or the probable," a deft way of describing the fiction writer's endless task of seeming to mirror reality (in most cases) while actually building her or his own world.

I read Aristotle's trenchant words with admiration and with the pleasing sense of getting a brief glimpse behind the veil of time—across twenty-four centuries I can see a man's mind at work—but I cannot say that I find them immediately useful when I sit down to write. Yes, of course our fictions need to be expressive of moral purpose, our characters to be consistently inconsistent. Yet here I am, beginning a new story, and here is Martine with her straight mousy hair and her narrow brown eyes. She shrugs; she turns. When is the rest of her going to show up?

Skipping over Castiglione's *The Book of the Courtier* and whatever wisdom Ruskin, Pater, and the Romantics have to offer, I went next to one of our best loved critical books, Forster's *Aspects of the Novel* (first published in 1927 and based on the lectures he delivered that spring at Trinity College, Cambridge). Forster by this time had written and published five novels, culminating in *A Passage to India* in 1924. He was writing as a critic, a reader, and a practitioner of fiction. Unlike his famous predecessor, he treats characters as being of paramount importance and devotes two of his ten chapters to them. "The main facts in human life," he tells us, "are five: birth, food, sleep, love and death . . . Let us briefly ask ourselves what part they play in our lives, and what in novels." We read along, nodding, feeling confident that we know how to answer his question. Yes, most authors spend more time on love than sleep, more time on death than food. Characters, Forster claims, "are real not because they are like ourselves . . . but because they are convincing," And, very important, "explicable." Although they may have secrets, the novelist knows everything about them. Whereas "[i]n daily life," he writes, "we never understand each other."

He goes on to give his famous account of round and flat characters. These definitions have so thoroughly entered our vocabulary, and are so frequently invoked, that to reread his original discussion is a startling experience. "The test of a round character," he writes, "is whether it is capable of surprising in a convincing way." His main example is Daniel Defoe's spirited adventuress, Moll Flanders, whom he describes as being like a single tree standing in the middle of a field. She fills the novel that bears her name in a very different way than, say, Emma Bovary or Anna Karenina.

The term "flat" nowadays is almost invariably disparaging, but this was not how Forster defined it. Indeed he takes issue with a critic who claims that flat characters, because they can be summed up in a single sentence, are a falsification of *homo fictus*. Forster agrees about the single sentence but goes on to argue that flat characters can achieve surprising depth. They have their antecedents, he explains, in the caricatures and humors of the seventeenth century and are created around a single idea:

It is a convenience for an author when he can strike with his full force at once, and flat characters are very useful to him, since they never need reintroducing, never run away, have not to be watched for development, and provide their own atmosphere—little luminous disks of a pre-arranged size, pushed hither and thither like counters across the void or between the stars; most satisfactory.

What Forster does not precisely say, but makes clear through this description, is that creating a good flat character is not conspicuously easier than creating a good round one. Look at all the things he wants a flat character to do: be instantly recognizable, be available at all times, provide their own atmosphere. Hackneyed details and dull prose are not going to metamorphose into a little luminous disk.

As an example he offers his splendid analysis of Lady Bertram, who appears in Jane Austen's third novel, *Mansfield Park*. Lady Bertram, he argues, is a very successful flat character, but when her two daughters get into trouble—the unmarried Julia elopes; the married Maria runs off with a lover—Lady Bertram rises to the occasion: "the disk has suddenly extended and become a little globe." And this, Forster explains, is part of Austen's genius; her flat characters are never conceived of as simply flat; they are always capable of reaching toward roundness. In conclusion, he offers an illuminating comparison between Austen and Dickens:

> Why do the characters in Jane Austen give us a slightly new pleasure each time they come in, as opposed to the merely repetitive pleasure that is caused by a character in Dickens? . . . the best reply is that her characters though smaller than his are more highly organized. They function all round, and even if her plot made greater demands on them than it does, they would still be adequate.

And here is the most crucial of Forster's demands for good flat characters. They should, if necessary, be able to respond to an emergency. We may be seeing them from only one angle, but nonetheless we have the pleasing sense that there are other angles, a more complicated history, just beyond the page.

I note too Forster's use of the word "organized." It is not the first word that most readers reach for in praise of character. "Vivid," "complex," "engaging," "lifelike," "poignant," "richly imagined"—these are the terms we use when we describe those characters who have taken up residence in our imaginations. But as writers facing the open page, none of these kindly descriptions is particularly useful in helping us to generate characters. "Organize" comes from the Greek word for "tool," and that is what our characters are: tools in the little laboratories of our stories. We make them and, ideally, they help us to make something else.

Searching my bookshelves, I found another author also using the term "organize" when referring to characters. Here is William H. Gass's beautiful and bracing close reading of a sentence from Henry James's *The Awkward Age*:

> "Mr. Cashmore, who would have been very redheaded if he had not been very bald, showed a single eyeglass and a long upper-lip; he was large and jaunty with little petulant movements and intense ejaculations that were not in the line of his type."

> We can imagine any number of other sentences about Mr. Cashmore added to this one. Now the question is: what is Mr. Cashmore? Here is the answer I shall give:

> Mr. Cashmore is (1) a noise, (2) a proper name, (3) a complex system of ideas, (4) a controlling conception, (5) an instrument of verbal organization, (6) a pretended mode of referring, and (7) a source of verbal energy. But Mr. Cashmore is not a person. He is not an object of perception, and nothing whatever that is appropriate to persons can be correctly said of him.

In the paragraphs that follow, Gass makes three persuasive points. First, Mr. Cashmore has the attributes that have been given to him, but he also has many others that have not been precisely ascribed. From what James tells us—the eyeglass, the baldness—we invent the rest. This is a crucial and complicated aspect of the relationship between readers and characters, and it is an aspect that authors are always seeking to manipulate in appropriate ways. How much, or how little, do we need to put on the page to persuade the reader to fill in the rest? Second, characters are those primary substances to which everything else in the novel is attached. And third, Gass argues for the importance of naming. Proper names, he says, are the only part of our prose whose meaning we invent for ourselves. "Character," he writes, "has a special excitement for a writer (apart from its organizing value) because it offers him a chance to give fresh meaning to new words." When I name a character Gemma, I am inventing the meaning of the word "Gemma."

I am not suggesting that we abandon *homo fictus*; indeed even Gass is unable to abandon him and soon lapses into gossiping about characters as if they were people—"What an unlikely couple"; "Who would have thought she'd end up being a car mechanic." But I do think something about this rather abstract discussion is both suggestive and helpful with regard to our difficulties in creating characters. Gass reminds us, on the one hand, how artificial characters are—they are constructs, not organic beings—and on the other, how rapidly, as readers, we respond to the right kind of verbal energy. Forster may think that Dickens's flat characters do not measure up to Austen's, but he remarks admiringly on Dickens's ability to "bounce" the reader into accepting even the most preposterous situations.

And Gass's emphasis on the importance of names also speaks to one of our more pervasive failures of imagination. At the beginning of a recent semester I compared my students' names to those of their characters. I was struck by how much more colorful, awkward, and memorable their own names were than those they bestowed on their characters. Looking through the pages of their fictions, I encountered Sarah after Rebecca, John after David. Of course there were exceptions, but many authors do tend to be remarkably conservative in their choice of names (which is not to say that every fictional world should be populated by characters named Twilight and Dogface).

We are, Gass insists, fully responsible for our characters—both for what Mr. Cashmore has been given and for what he hasn't—and when we create a new character we are inventing a new language. As lexicographers, we cannot take too much for granted. It is up to us to provide both connotation and denotation. In stories where the character is unnamed readers still count on the author to create their own definition for whichever pronoun identifies the protagonist: she, he, we, they, you, and, over and over again, I.

❁

These venerable works offer many insights but few practical suggestions. Happily, recent decades have seen the publication of dozens of how-to and advice books, which deal with creating characters in a more pragmatic fashion. Lists of specific suggestions and questions are offered—Does your character have a nickname? What is her or his horoscope? Does she or he have a job? Or hobbies?—and strategies are recommended. Yes, yes, I think as I read these sensible remarks, written by and for writers, but when I close the book and try to apply the suggestions, my own characters still seem to divide not into the desirable round and flat, but the barely breathing and roadkill (to borrow some categories from Francine Prose). Perhaps the real difficulty is that the first readers for whom we need to bring our characters to life are ourselves, and these lists and strategies, although very helpful with the later stages of creation, may not help to ignite that first vital spark. We have a hard time believing that simply declaring that Ted, often known as Lefty, is a Leo who has recently taken up salsa dancing and enjoys his job working as a railway brakeman can result in a vivid, well-organized character.

Still, there is something irresistible about lists and, over the years, I have come up with my own collection of prompts, rules, and admonitions for creating characters:

PROMPTS

- Name the character.
- Use myself, or someone I know.
- Borrow from a newspaper story.
- Give the character a house/flat/doorway/car that I know well.
- Send her to a career counselor.

- Let her talk.
- Make her act (n.b. Aristotle).
- Give a sense of her role and position in her family, and in society.
- Show her relationships—we may all die alone but hardly anyone lives alone.
- Describe her appearance, insofar as it's relevant.

RULES

- "Good" characters must have some failure or vice: bad handwriting, a hatred of violets.
- "Bad" characters must have some strength or virtue: perfect pitch, the ability to recognize edible mushrooms.
- Every character should have something she shares with me: a landscape, a habit, a taste.
- Every character should have something I absolutely do not share: perfect pitch, the ability to recognize edible mushrooms.
- If the character is a stereotype—the bad sister, the absentminded professor—be sure to make her not *only* a stereotype.

ADMONITIONS

· When creating a character very different
from myself I often need to create her
or him from the outside. I give the character a house, a job, activities, friends,
clothes, and, in the course of doing so, I
gradually figure out her or his inner life.

· Clones and doppelgangers, those
characters who stand in for me, or who
I want the reader to believe do so, I
create from the inside out. I know her
desires, her dislikes, her dreams, and
gradually I figure out where she lives
and whether she has a bank balance.

The rules about having something in common
with me and something I absolutely do not share are
ones I find especially helpful. I need solid ground to
stand on while I invent a character. But for that character to really come to life, my imagination must be
engaged, so I give the character something—a taste, an
activity, a relationship, a phobia—quite foreign to me
so that I can imagine them into being. What would it
be like to hate violets?

In an interview about his novel *Independence Day*,
Richard Ford made a passionate claim for the virtues

of the imagination. Frank Bascombe, the narrator of Ford's novel, is to a large extent defined by the death of his son and his subsequent divorce. Ford, who has never had a child or been divorced, when pressed about his relationship to Bascombe's life, said the following:

> Invented it. That's my job, I think. I didn't do these things and yet I try to write vividly about them. That in itself is a testament to the vitality, the immense possibility of imaginative fiction. I am sometimes vexed by people wanting to trace back something that I write to some fact in my autobiography. It sells short something that I so believe in, something that is so important a resource to human nature, namely an ability to invent something better than you know.

I love this praise of the imagination, yet, as a matter of craft, I would point out that Ford and Bascombe do share some aspects of autobiography. Bascombe lives in New Jersey, a landscape Ford knows well, and he used to earn his living as a sportswriter, a job Ford held in his late thirties.

✿

While these helpful lists may guide us in discovering our characters, the question remains: What brings a character to life for a reader? Let us look at how a number of authors introduce their characters. Here is the opening of O'Connor's masterful story "Revelation":

> The doctor's waiting room, which was very small, was almost full when the Turpins entered and Mrs. Turpin, who was very large, made it look even smaller by her presence. She stood looming at the head of the magazine table set in the center of it, a living demonstration that the room was inadequate and ridiculous. Her little bright black eyes took in all the patients as she sized up the seating situation. There was one vacant chair and a place on the sofa occupied by a blond child in a dirty blue romper. . . .

Like Mr. Cashmore, Mrs. Turpin has only a few physical attributes: her size, her little bright black eyes. She has a wonderful proper name; she has a ruling conception; she is an instrument of verbal organization and a source of verbal energy. She also has, and I think we can glean this even from a few sentences, what she *hasn't* been given. We amplify her size; we guess her wardrobe. From the moment Mrs. Turpin is introduced, in that beautifully cadenced first sentence, we know that her job is to make the world seem smaller; she marches into that waiting room and the reader's imagination. The crucial thing that brings Mrs. Turpin to life, though, is no single attribute or detail, no action or remark, but the overwhelming sense we get, as we read these lines, of how Mrs. Turpin regards herself and the world: her attitude.

This seems the key to creating memorable characters. It is also, I think, the reason why doing so can prove such a tricky task. No amount of detail—eyes, teeth, hair, jobs, dreams, relationship to mother, history of dog ownership, horoscope—will avail unless it conveys attitude. Indeed, long lists of detail without affect may simply make the task of imagining the character harder, for both writer and reader. What one needs are the right details, the so-called *telling* details—and what those details *tell* is attitude.

O'Connor sets a splendid example in these endeavors. Her characters, especially her three great archetypes—the older woman who knows where she stands, e.g., Mrs. Turpin and the mother in "Everything That Rises Must Converge"; the righteous younger person, e.g., Hulga in "Good Country People"; and the ne'er-do-well young man, e.g., The Misfit in "A Good Man Is Hard to Find"—are brimming with attitude. We always know how she or he would enter a room.

But I am not sure that O'Connor is an entirely helpful model, perhaps because her characters, playing their parts in her melodramatic plots, tend toward the extreme. Her accomplishment is clear, but not one that most writers should seek to emulate. Picture, for instance, Mrs. Turpin showing up in one of Alice Munro's wonderful stories. She would not just fill the room, but empty it.

In looking for a more helpful model, I turned to "Polly Ongle," a novella by the Canadian writer John Metcalf:

> Paul was enraged by his son's appearance, manners, attitudes, reflex hostility, hobbies and habits. He was reduced to incoherent anger by the boy's having mutilated all his clothes by inserting zippers in legs and sleeves, zippers which were secured by bicycle padlocks, so that he looked like an emaciated scarecrow constructed by a sexual deviant . . . by his bleached hair which he coloured at weekends with purple food-dye, by his ruminant of a girlfriend . . . by

> his intense ignorance of everything that
> had happened prior to 1970, by his inex-
> plicable and seemingly inexhaustible sup-
> ply of ready cash . . .

And on and on, as the narrator offers Paul's seemingly inexhaustible list of things he finds aggravating
about his son. The sharply specific, mostly trivial details reveal the attitudes of both characters toward a
whole range of things: clothes, money, history, themselves, and each other.

For me a useful aspect of Metcalf's characterization
is Paul's grumpiness. A number of writers I know write
monologues as a way to bring a character to life, but
often I have some difficulty in getting my characters to
hold forth. Even my chattiest teenager, my most eloquent carpenter, grows oddly speechless, as if she or he
were suddenly being forced to make conversation on a
bare stage before a hostile audience. "Polly Ongle," however, provides a fruitful model. When I set my characters
on each other, allow them not simply to talk but to rant
about each other's shortcomings, I tend to get much
better results. What Flora couldn't stand about Edward,
I write, was his too-short trousers, the way he was always apologizing for the weather, his insistence on using
a fork in a Chinese restaurant, his inability to decide to

see a film the same day he read a review, etc. Maybe it's a sign of my own bad nature that grumpiness generates more energy than affection, at least on the page.

But affection *can* generate energy, as Truman Capote shows in "A Christmas Memory." Like O'Connor and Metcalf, Capote is a master of the telling detail. Here is the narrator describing his elderly cousin. "In addition to never having seen a movie, she has never: eaten in a restaurant, traveled more than five miles from home, received or sent a telegram, read anything except funny pages and the Bible, worn cosmetics, cursed, wished someone harm." A vivid picture of the cousin emerges from this list of all the things she has never done. Perhaps in part because of that convention by which readers understand that more of a character is implied than stated—Mrs. Turpin notices the child's dirty blue romper; we guess that she herself is nicely dressed—it can be particularly powerful to spell out, as Capote does, what a character would never own, or do, or say, or dream. Such statements, whether made by or on behalf of our characters, almost invariably convey attitude.

❈

Implicitly I have been discussing the creation of round characters, but the successful flat character is also endowed with attitude. Remember Lady Bertram grieving over her daughters' behavior? Those little luminous disks are disks with attitude; that's why the reader remembers them from one appearance to the next and instantly recognizes them. And precisely because of this a successful flat character can, if necessary, expand into roundness. If we stopped reading after the first paragraph of "Revelation," Mrs. Turpin would merely be a superb flat character, but if we continue, then we see O'Connor take her heroine's hopes and fears to an entirely new level. Mrs. Turpin's sense of self, which depends so much on her sense of where she stands in society, is deepened and complicated and finally enlarged to include her tremendous apocalyptic vision of heaven.

This consanguinity between round and flat is, I think, one reason why a story like John Cheever's "The Swimmer" works so well. As Cheever's main character, Neddy, swims home across the county through the swimming pools of various old friends, acquaintances, and neighbors, we are introduced to a stunning array of flat characters. My favorites are the Hallorans: "an elderly couple of enormous wealth who seemed to bask in the suspicion that they might be Communists. They were zealous reformers but they were not Communists, and . . . for reasons that had never been explained to him [they] did not wear bathing suits."

As the protagonist of the story, Neddy ought to be a round character, but I am not sure that he is, or at least not in the conventional sense. Apart from his relentless swimming and his snobbishness, Neddy is largely lacking in attitude. Instead what brings him to life are the reactions of the many flat characters he encounters on his journey and also, it is worth noting, Cheever's remarkable descriptions of the swimming pools. But Neddy himself remains curiously blank. The triumph of the story is to circumnavigate that blankness, like a black hole, as it drives toward its famous conclusion.

Perhaps what Neddy most fully embodies is Aristotle's dictum that character is action. From the opening page of the story, he is *in* action, and what he does both delights and intrigues us. There's a wonderful comic pleasure in the idea, and the actuality (if I may use such a word in connection with "The Swimmer"), of Neddy's journey across his home state. He comes to life for us not only because of his telling relationships with his neighbors but also because of the unusual task in which we find him engaged. Of course not every story can be organized around a single activity; still there is something to be learned about the degree to which our vision of a major character can be governed by the attitudes of minor characters. We might call this "the Great Gatsby effect."

Thinking more about attitude, on behalf of both round and flat characters, I realized that it can be conveyed in different ways. Here is Chekhov introducing his protagonist Gurov in the story "The Lady with the Dog":

> He was not yet forty, but he had a twelve-year-old daughter and two sons in school. He had married young, while still a second-year student, and now his wife seemed half again his age. She was a tall woman with dark eyebrows, erect, imposing, dignified, and a thinking person, as she called herself. . . He secretly considered her none too bright, narrow-minded, graceless, was afraid of her, and disliked being home. He had begun to be unfaithful long ago, was unfaithful often, and, probably for that reason, almost always spoke ill of women, and when they were discussed in his presence, he would say of them:
>
> "An inferior race!"

We learn a good deal in this paragraph about Gurov and how he sees himself and the world; in the process of conveying this information, the prose takes a back seat. The writing has a quiet confidence and authority but it does not draw attention to itself. The details, although precise and subtle, are not distinctively different from those that many other writers might offer in such a description.

Here, in a very different vein, is the opening of the "Autumn" section in Toni Morrison's first novel, *The Bluest Eye*:

> Nuns go by as quiet as lust, and drunken men with sober eyes sing in the lobby of the Greek hotel. Rosemary Villanucci, our next-door friend who lives above her father's café, sits in a 1939 Buick eating bread and butter. She rolls down the window to tell my sister Frieda and me that we can't come in. We stare at her, wanting her bread, but more than that wanting to poke the arrogance out of her eyes and smash the pride of ownership that curls her chewing mouth. When she comes out of the car we will beat her up, make red marks on her white skin, and she will cry and ask us do we want her to pull her pants down.

From the first sentence, with its startling juxtapositions—nuns and lust, drunken men and sober eyes—we recognize a torqued poetry. The prose is stepping forward, demanding our attention. As we continue reading, we understand, both through the details and the syntax, that we are in the presence of a young narrator who is creating her world through unmediated experiences. She is going to invite us to share them, rather than analyze them.

Also important to note is how Morrison announces her narrator's race. By and large at the moment, in North America, readers tend to assume that unless otherwise stated characters are white and/or share the race of their authors. Morrison, writing in the late sixties, uses the phrase "her white skin" to alert her readers to the fact that her narrator is not white. Deeper into the novel, many other details confirm that Claudia is black. In my most recent novel I have two characters of color. I indicate that Merrie is black only once—readers might miss it—but I hope they won't miss her moral insight. A second character was, in my imagination, Korean, but he appears so briefly that my attempts to describe his race came across as merely racist. Now his race isn't mentioned and so, by default—see both assumptions above—he is white in the minds of most readers. If there is ever a film of the novel, I will plead for him to appear as his true self. The assumptions around these issues are shifting all the time. Writing forty years after Morrison,

Teju Cole, in his novel *Open City*, confirms the race of his narrator almost in an aside after thirty pages. "It was an anger that, I couldn't help feeling, was partly directed at me, the only other African in the room." He then adds that he was Nigerian.

Morrison's prose demonstrates what I would call "embodied attitude": a combination of her details, her diction, and her syntax. I would ascribe this same quality to other voice-driven writers: Sandra Cisneros, Lydia Davis, Junot Díaz, William Faulkner, Leonard Michaels, and Grace Paley come to mind. In "A Conversation with My Father," Paley writes: "My father is eighty-six years old and in bed. His heart, that bloody motor, is equally old and will not do certain jobs anymore. It still floods his head with brainy light. But it won't let his legs carry the weight of his body around the house." The details may be commonplace yet her choice of adjectives—"bloody," "brainy"—makes us immediately aware that here, as Forster said about the Alexandrian poet C. P. Cavafy, is someone standing at a slight angle to the universe. Whether a writer chooses to foreground voice, or to convey attitude in other ways, seems to be one of those choices that writers make so instinctively that it doesn't feel like a choice. The task remains the same: to give, show, create, describe, embody *attitude*.

My characters are still showing up in my early drafts with their brown hair and blue eyes. Fully aware of how uninformative these traits are, I let them stand as place markers until I can find the right details, the telling details. And as I search for them, I try to be attentive to both what the real world of constantly changing secrets and the world of fiction can teach me. What writers need to get on the page is how their characters feel about themselves and about their family, friends, coworkers, strangers, and enemies; what matters to them and what doesn't. Seen in that light all those lists—phobias, favorite food, astrological sign, hobbies, political beliefs—can be immensely helpful. In "Revelation" Mrs. Turpin never does consult her horoscope, but somehow I feel I know precisely what it would be like if she were to do so.

NOTHING BUT HIMSELF

Embracing Jane Austen's Second Chances

SEVERAL SPRINGS AGO I made a long overdue pilgrimage to Winchester Cathedral. Inside the main door I asked a guide for directions to Jane Austen's grave. As she pointed across the church, she apologized for the lack of flowers. They were not permitted during Lent. "But during the rest of the year," she assured me, "you can find her grave by the flowers. People are always bringing Jane bouquets." Austen moved to Winchester in May 1817 to be closer to the surgeon who was going to cure her and spent the last weeks of her short life there. She dictated her final poem on July 15 and died on July 18, 1817; she was forty-one years old. She is buried in the north aisle of the nave and her grave has not one but two markers. The older one, the stone slab in the floor, contains no mention of her work but praises "[t]he benevolence of her heart, the sweetness of her temper, and the extraordinary endowments of her mind." Nearby, a bronze plaque on the wall praises her novels. Reading these touching inscriptions, I thought how typical the guide's remark was of the affection that Austen, and her work, inspire. People who love her novels also cherish her and her uneventful life: Dear Jane. She is buried not far from a casket said to contain the bones of King Canute, the great eleventh-century Viking king who helped to convert England to Christianity.

There are no kings in Austen's work. Her six novels, as she herself was among the first to comment, revolve around a limited set of concerns, are set in small communities, and are comedic rather than tragic. Her plots are mostly predictable, although she is certainly capable of surprises (see Louisa's famous fall from the Cobb in Lyme, or Emma's rudeness to Miss Bates). As for her characters, she has, like Flannery O'Connor, certain types to which she steadfastly returns: the foolish parent, the misguided daughter, the social climber, the easily overlooked estimable young woman, the reserved man of integrity. These flat characters show up in book after book, and for the most part, although they contribute to the events of the narrative, remain unchanged by them. Only her major characters—the heroine and the hero—are transformed by the last page.

I first encountered Austen's work at the age of fourteen, when I read *Pride and Prejudice* for school. At the time, I lived in a community that Austen herself, in some parallel universe, might have relished as subject matter: the boys' boarding school in Scotland where my father taught and where first my mother, and then my stepmother, was the nurse. The school was situated in the valley of Glenalmond, ten slow miles from the nearest town. We knew what it was like to deal with the same small number of people week after week, year after year; to have a keen sense of hierarchy: first came the headmaster, then his deputy, then the bursar, then the housemasters. All of them came before my father, who was only a regular master, but he could look down on the groundsmen. We also knew what it was like to have occasional visitors who called that hierarchy into question.

But seeing the world around me mirrored, however obliquely, was not part of the original appeal of *Pride and Prejudice.* I read to escape my environment, and made no connection between Austen's social milieu and my own (although I would have welcomed one of her balls happening nearby). Nor could I have explained at that time—I had yet to read E. M. Forster's analysis in *Aspects of the Novel*—exactly why her characters gave me such pleasure. Compared with those in, say, *Wuthering Heights*, they are painfully sedate. No one promises to love anyone from beyond the grave. No suitor threatens to break every bone in another's body. But there was this feeling of something moving beneath the surface of Austen's calm prose that made me, even as I finished the book, want to turn back to the opening page.

Decades later, I still find myself struggling to understand what makes her novels so alluring, and what I can learn from her work. I gained new insight when I decided to follow, humbly, in her footsteps and write a romance titled *Banishing Verona*. I had finally published *Eva Moves the Furniture*, a novel based on my mother's life, and I was anxious to return to purely imaginary territory. I also liked the idea of writing in a form that had recognizable rules and that offered the possibility of a happy ending. Among the rules governing romances, I would suggest the following:

1. The lovers are unlikely in some obvious way.
2. They meet early and are then separated—either physically or emotionally—for most of the narrative.
3. There must be significant obstacles—dragons and demons—to be overcome.

4. Changes of setting, even from drawing room to street, are vital for revealing the characters and moving the narrative forward.

5. Many minor characters will assist the lovers on their journey.

6. A subplot, or two, is required to keep the lovers apart, to allow time to pass, to act as a foil to the main plot, and to entertain the reader.

Crucially, the reader must come to feel that this romance is not merely a matter of personal preference between two people, but that a whole world order is in question until the two find each other. In offering these criteria, I do not mean to suggest that Austen herself consciously devised or followed such guidelines, only that they emerge from her body of work—part of the web she weaves to ensnare her readers—and have been followed by many other authors in the two centuries since her death.

In speaking of Austen's lovers, I use the verb "find" deliberately. Although her characters go on the most modest of journeys—never more than an hour or two on foot or a few hours by carriage—we end up feel-ing that they have covered a long distance in her short novels. They travel from a place where the self and others are poorly known—mendacity is mistaken for integrity; attraction for antipathy—to a place where the self is seen and understood. (Austen herself made this journey, perhaps more than once. At the age of twenty-seven, she accepted Harris Bigg-Wither's proposal one evening, celebrated the news with family and friends, and the following morning told her suitor that she had changed her mind.) The couple does not so much decide upon as discover each other and, in the course of their discovery, something profound is revealed. Austen knew Shakespeare well and must surely have appreciated that archetypal romance, *A Midsummer Night's Dream*, in which the lovers wander into the forest, are separated, reconfigured, and finally reunited.

But she herself does not go in for forests, any more than for kings. She is committed to her version of realism, and nowhere, I would argue, is that commitment more obvious than in her last novel, *Persuasion*, which was published posthumously. In lesser romances, the flaws of the protagonist vanish and the virtues are exaggerated, but here Austen achieves a compelling love story that comes out of a hard-won negotiation with the rules of her world. Again I think of the Brontës, in whose work love conquers all and good looks and/or virtue make up for lack of social standing or income.

Persuasion offers no such sweeping passions but rather two characters no longer in the first ardor of youth— Anne Elliot and Captain Wentworth—grappling with their own flaws and those of their society.

In balancing the demands of realism with those of romance, Austen must do battle with her readers. Just as we will complete a character's appearance—we give Mr. Cashmore his eyes, Mrs. Turpin her wardrobe—so we also long to complete their lives by making sure that they live happily ever after. From the reader's point of view, it is a truth universally acknowledged that if a single man and a single woman are in the same story, they are going to end up together. This ardent matchmaking has, as Austen seems to have known all along, and I painfully discovered, several repercussions for the writer. In their eagerness to unite characters, readers tend to be oblivious to such quotidian concerns as class, money, family, and, to a surprising degree, appearance. Readers of *Jane Eyre* invariably side with small, poor, plain Jane and dislike the woman cast as her possible rival: the wealthy Blanche with her magnificent shoulders. I was both making use of, and making fun of, these biases in my novel *Banishing Verona* when I made my twenty-nine-year-old hero look like a Raphael angel and my thirty-seven-year-old heroine resemble the famous bust of Beethoven. (Verona's advanced age was a little nod to Anne Elliot.) I knew that, almost irrespective of the difficulties with which I burdened my characters, readers would be expecting this unlikely couple to end up together. The question was how to manage those expectations, and delay realizing them, without causing either boredom or frustration.

Here Austen sets a wonderful example in both plot and prose. At fourteen I was too young to recognize that, while I thought I was reading *Pride and Prejudice* to see who married whom, I was really reading for the unswerving music of Austen's sentences, which, from first to last, carry the reader effortlessly along. In this, and in all her novels, she creates narrators who conjure up her characters so knowingly and so intelligently that we are beguiled even by the most snobbish and the most foolish. Her work single-handedly contradicts Henry James's famous description of novels as "large, loose, baggy monsters" and Randall Jarrell's much quoted: "The novel is a prose narrative of some length that has something wrong with it."

Selfishly, when I began to write my own fiction, I was glad to learn that *Pride and Prejudice* had not sprung full-blown onto the page, but was the product of hard work, deep thought, and revision. An early version under the title "First Impressions" was rejected by a publisher in 1797. Not until 1813, after she had published *Sense and Sensibility* (also the product of much revision), did Austen publish *Pride and Prejudice* to great acclaim. In the case of *Persuasion*, she finished the novel, wrote "Finis" on the last page, and then, over the next few weeks, rewrote the ending to give us the now-cherished proposal scene between Anne and Wentworth.

Paragraph by paragraph, I do not think that *Persuasion* offers quite the lustrous pleasure of her earlier work. The novel is more complicated in tone, less steady in voice, and sometimes a bit plodding. I would feel like a heretic saying this if Virginia Woolf did not make almost the same claim. "There is," Woolf writes in *The Common Reader*, "a peculiar beauty and a peculiar dullness in *Persuasion*. The dullness is that which so often marks the transition stage between two periods. The writer is a little bored. She has grown too familiar with the ways of her world . . . But, while we feel that Jane Austen has done this before, and done it better, we also feel that she is trying to do something which she has never yet attempted . . . She is beginning to discover that the world is larger, more mysterious, and more romantic than she had supposed." Perhaps this is why I find rereading the novel such a perplexing experience. I fret over sentences; I get cross when I see the wheels turning, or the same note hit too often, or a character behaving badly in familiar ways. And yet, when I reach the last page, I discover that the novel, from first to last, is once again complete and shimmering in my imagination. *Persuasion* is one of those rare works that becomes much more than the sum of its sentences. If the reader helps to create the text, then the author also helps to create the reader, and in her last novel Austen creates readers who are more intelligent, more compassionate, and more empathetic than most of us are in real life.

Her poor health—she was already in the grip of what would turn out to be her last illness—may have contributed to these lapses. But I like to think that Woolf's analysis is correct; many of the novel's shortcomings stem from Austen's desire to sail into uncharted waters. *Persuasion* begins not with the arrival of an eligible man but with his return. The main event in the world of an Austen novel—the proposal—has already occurred. Seven years ago Anne accepted Wentworth only to break off their engagement, thus making them a perfect example of an unlikely couple. The two are separated by their history, by Wentworth's anger and by Anne's perception, shared by those around her, that, at twenty-seven, she is too old for love. Austen is both keeping and reinventing the rules of the form she has mastered so well.

She manages Wentworth's reappearance, and her plot in general, with her usual keen understanding of the importance of money. The novel opens with Anne's father, Sir Walter, at last being persuaded to rent out the family seat, Kellynch Hall, in order to pay off his debts. His tenant turns out to be none other than Admiral Croft, the brother-in-law of Anne's long-ago suitor. We learn how, after "a short period of exquisite felicity," Anne ended the engagement largely at the urging of her mother's friend Lady Russell. Wentworth was poor; his prospects were uncertain; his temperament was headstrong. The reader may be outraged by these considerations and Lady Russell—watching Anne remain single year after year—has come to regret her own advice, but Anne herself has a more complicated view. Even if Lady Russell was wrong, she, as a motherless girl of nineteen, was right to do what her older friend urged. "I should," she tells Wentworth at the end of the novel, "have suffered more in continuing in the engagement than I did even in giving it up." When Wentworth first proposes, he has nothing to recommend him but himself, and that is not enough for Lady Russell, or, perhaps, for Austen. By the time he proposes again at the end of the novel, he has a good fortune, good connections, and a good career. Love needs the things of this world.

The opening pages of the novel also introduce another important theme: the relationship between life and books. The only book, we are told, that Sir Walter enjoys reading, under any and all circumstances, is the Baronetage. He has already edited his own entry to make it more accurate, and he wishes he could make further changes involving his older daughter, the almost equally vain and foolish Elizabeth. *Persuasion* is often said to be about second chances, but to my mind it is more about revision. What use are second chances if we don't learn to see and act differently? Our star-crossed lovers, Anne and Captain Wentworth, find themselves in each other's company less than a quarter of the way through the novel, but initially Wentworth seems to see Anne in much the same way as her father and sisters do: "only Anne," a counterpart to his "nothing but himself."

The renting of Kellynch Hall forces almost all the main characters to move to new settings. While Sir Walter and Elizabeth go to Bath and Admiral and Mrs. Croft move into Kellynch Hall, Anne makes the small but significant journey to Uppercross to help her younger sister, Mary, who is married to Charles Musgrove. A few weeks later Wentworth visits the Crofts and begins to pay attention to Charles's sisters: the lively Henrietta and Louisa. I note with admiration the masterstroke of giving Anne two rivals, multiplying the dragons she must slay and obscuring Wentworth's feelings.

In *The Art of Fiction* John Gardner argues that there are only two great plots: the stranger comes to town, or the hero goes on a journey. In *Persuasion* Austen skillfully employs both. Having forced Anne to leave home once, she now sends her on a second journey. Along with Mary, Charles, Charles's sisters, and Captain Wentworth, she dispatches her to the seaside town of Lyme. "The young people," she tells us in a surprisingly modern idiom, "were all wild to see Lyme." (In my novel, lacking both Austen's constraints and her finesse, I dispatched my characters to America.)

The new setting reveals new aspects of the characters we already know, and ushers in a second group of the minor characters that Austen deploys so skillfully throughout the novel. The climax of the visit to Lyme is Louisa's fall from the Cobb, the seawall. Captain Wentworth has been heard, by both Anne and Louisa, praising firmness of character; one should never, he claims, change one's mind. Now Louisa, determined to prove her firmness, insists on being jumped down the stairs from the Cobb by Wentworth not once but twice. On the second occasion she jumps too soon, he fails to catch her, and she falls lifeless to the pavement. While everyone else, including Wentworth, is undone by Louisa's accident, Anne rises to the occasion; she sends for a surgeon, and directs the others to carry Louisa to the inn. Reading this vivid scene, I think of Aristotle's claim that character is action. Now, at last, Anne has a chance to act.

Subplots, always important in a romance, are particularly so in *Persuasion* because we are all pretending to ignore the main plot: the possible reunion of Anne and Wentworth. The visit to Lyme introduces two suspenseful and useful subplots. A fellow guest at the inn where Anne and the others are staying turns out to be Sir Walter's heir. Years ago Mr. Elliot spurned Sir Walter's overtures, but now he shows a marked interest in Anne. The twenty-seven-year-old Miss Elliot is suddenly attracting admirers! Another subplot concerns Captain Benwick, who was engaged to the sister of Wentworth's friend Captain Harville. (The novel brims with naval officers.) But his fiancée died while he was at sea; Benwick is staying in Lyme with the Harvilles, apparently in deep mourning. His presence allows Austen to question the nature of fidelity in love and to continue to explore the connection between life and reading; each will prove vital in the proposal scene. Meanwhile Captain and Mrs. Harville reinforce what Admiral and Mrs. Croft have already demonstrated: naval officers make for unusually good husbands.

Everyone in the novel is worried about Louisa—as they should be—but I, as a reader, am not. So skillfully has Austen rearranged the world order that the life of a young woman is of less importance than what happens between the two thwarted lovers. Besides, I am in a world more comedic than tragic; I know that Louisa's fall is the far frontier of violence in an Austen novel. My lack of concern in no way diminishes the effect of these wonderful pages and of all that they reveal about the characters.

I will not explore in detail Austen's skillful management of the second half of the novel, when most of the characters move to yet another new setting—the town of Bath—but I do want to remark on her introducing an additional subplot in the form of Anne's old school friend, Mrs. Smith, whom widowhood has left with nothing but herself. Like Mr. Elliot and Captain Benwick, Mrs. Smith enters the novel naturally and allows us to, once again, appreciate Anne's virtues. But her real job is to let us know what lies behind Mr. Elliot's sudden interest in Sir Walter and Anne. Austen pays a surprising amount of attention to this part of the plot. While Anne and Wentworth's past is dealt with in a brisk three pages and the many events of the visit to Lyme are compressed into nineteen, she now, close to the end of the novel, devotes an entire

chapter—sixteen pages—to a single conversation between Anne and Mrs. Smith.

And what a roller coaster the conversation is. It takes
place on the morning after the momentous concert at
which Anne has realized that Wentworth still, again,
cares for her. Mrs. Smith asks for details of the evening.
She is convinced that Anne is all but engaged to Mr. Elliot and at first refuses to accept her denials. "It is a thing
of course among us, that every man is refused—till he
offers . . . Let me plead for my—present friend I cannot call him, but for my former friend. Where can you
look for a more suitable match? Where could you expect
a more gentlemanlike, agreeable man? Let me recommend Mr. Elliot." In her anxiety to refuse the recom-
mendation Anne at last lets slip that her interests lie elsewhere. Only then does Mrs. Smith reveal that, although
he was her husband's closest friend, Mr. Elliot has failed
her in her widowhood, and that his first marriage was
made solely for money. Having become wealthy, he is
now vitally interested in inheriting the baronetcy, hence
his renewed attentions to Sir Walter.

Anne is glad to have her friend's confidence, distressed to learn about her difficulties, and understandably bewildered by her initial praise of Mr. Elliot. When
she inquires about this last, Mrs. Smith replies, "My
dear . . . there was nothing to be done. I considered your

84

marrying him as certain, though he might not yet have made the offer, and I could no more speak the truth of him, than if he had been your husband." Surely it is no accident that in the next paragraph Anne's thoughts turn to her other unreliable "advisor." Lady Russell, enthralled by Mr. Elliot's good manners, would like nothing more than to see Anne marry him and "It was just possible that she might have been persuaded . . . !" No wonder Anne determines that she "never should, in any circumstance of tolerable similarity, give such advice." In all of this Austen is following yet another major rule of the romance novel: mistakes are made, misunderstandings occur, reputation and reality are confused.

Now, at last, the way is clear for the lovers to find each other. In the first version of the proposal that she wrote, the one followed by "Finis," Austen brought Anne and Captain Wentworth together and allowed them, almost immediately, to reach an understanding. In the revision—the ending as we know it—she writes a much more complicated scene in which, rather than leave the two lovers alone, she has them address each other in the presence of, and through, various intermediaries. Two days after the concert Anne arrives at the Musgroves' lodgings to find, at one end of the drawing room, Mrs. Musgrove and Mrs. Croft discussing the folly of long engagements. Meanwhile at the other end

Captain Harville is talking to Captain Wentworth. As Anne approaches, Wentworth sits down at a nearby table to write a letter. Harville summons her to the window. There he shows her a portrait of Captain Benwick that had originally been painted for his sister. Now Benwick has, tactlessly, commissioned him to get it reset for his new fiancée. Wentworth, he tells Anne, is writing about the business.

Benwick's sudden swerve from mourning to new romance leads to a debate between Anne and Harville as to which gender is most constant in affection; they each argue, in passionate detail, for their own. Harville claims that men's feelings are, like their physiques, more robust; Anne, using the same analogy, claims that those of women are more tender. But given the danger, toil, and privations that men endure, she goes on, it is just as well that they are not also burdened with womanly feelings. All the while, as they go back and forth, Wentworth is sitting nearby, writing. When at last he and Harville set out on their errand, he manages to get the letter into Anne's hands. It turns out to have nothing to do with Benwick's portrait and everything to do with his feelings for her.

At last, in the streets of Bath, the two lovers find each other and are able to talk freely. Wentworth confesses that he had been angry with Anne, and had tried to attach himself to Louisa. But "[a]t Lyme he had received lessons of more than one sort. The passing admiration of Mr. Elliot had at least roused him, and the scenes on the Cobb, and at Captain Harville's, had fixed her superiority." Then, to his dismay, he had discovered that others considered him an engaged man. He fled Lyme, hoping to weaken both his relationship with Louisa and other people's perceptions of it. What narrow escapes the lovers have had. And now they have found each other.

Persuasion does, as Woolf said, show Austen doing things she has done before, but it also shows her moving into new territory, "discovering that the world is larger, more mysterious and more romantic than she had supposed." The most dramatic shift is not in Anne's age or her situation but in the freedom with which Austen gives voice to her tumultuous feelings. From the moment Captain Wentworth reappears, she is aware of him, and the reader is privy to that awareness with wonderful immediacy. But only after months of misunderstandings, when they at last attend the concert I have already mentioned, do Anne and Wentworth finally talk. In the aftermath of their conversation Austen writes:

> Anne saw nothing, thought nothing of the brilliancy of the room. Her happiness was from within. Her eyes were bright, and

her cheeks glowed; but she knew nothing about it. She was thinking only of the last half hour, and as they passed to their seats, her mind took a hasty range over it . . . His opinion of Louisa Musgrove's inferiority, an opinion which he had seemed solicitous to give, his wonder at Captain Benwick, his feelings as to a first, strong attachment; sentences begun which he could not finish, his half averted eyes and more than half expressive glance,—all, all declared that he had a heart returning to her at least; that anger, resentment, avoidance, were no more; and that they were succeeded, not merely by friendship and regard, but by the tenderness of the past. Yes, some share of the tenderness of the past. She could not contemplate the changes as implying less. He must love her.

The paragraph shows Anne both thinking and feeling her way to those last four wonderful words. She is not someone who changes her mind on a whim. Here we see her assembling the evidence, proving to herself that what she has hoped for, ever since Wentworth reappeared, is in fact the case. A few pages later a second insight is revealed with equal force. "Jealousy of Mr. Elliot! It was the only intelligible motive. Captain Wentworth jealous of her affection! Could she have believed it a week ago,—three hours ago! For a moment the gratification was exquisite." The writing in these scenes—the sentence fragments, the jagged, conflicting emotions, the sensation of almost too many feelings crowding into a single moment—paved the way for the accomplishments of George Eliot, Henry James, Woolf herself, and many others, in portraying the inner lives of their characters.

The rules of romance novels offer particular freedom to a writer, but the form is also beset with dangers. While readers almost invariably engage in ardent matchmaking, they are also quick to judge heterosexual love as slight, or unworthy, subject matter. In *Aspects of the Novel* Forster ponders why novelists spend what he judges to be an unnatural amount of time on love. He suspects this stems from the unduly sensitive state of mind the novelist enters when in the throes of composition. I myself think that the appeal of romance has much more to do with the possibilities for bad behavior. As for readers' contradictory responses, I attribute them to several factors. One that seems particularly relevant to *Persuasion* is the apparently random nature of love, both in its early stages and its later outcome. Austen embraces that randomness on behalf of her minor characters—Louisa falls off the Cobb, out of one relationship and into another—but her hero and heroine are held to more stringent standards. Readers have been hoping for most of the novel that Anne and Captain Wentworth will be reunited, but what makes this ending so satisfying is not merely our partisan feelings, but our sense that these characters have, over the course of the novel, slain various dragons—Louisa! Mr. Elliot!—and remained true to themselves while honoring the strict mores of the period. Captain Wentworth, who earlier seemed ready to settle for any obliging young woman, now recognizes that only Anne's superior nature can answer his needs. Bravely—and this takes as much courage as embarking on a stormy voyage—he risks a second rejection. As for Anne, she has become a woman who recognizes both the truth of her own affections and the inescapable foolishness of the father and sister she must leave behind in order to claim her place in the world. There is nothing random about their union.

In his conversation with Anne, Captain Harville argues that women are the inconstant sex, fickle in their affections and soon forgetting. Anne protests: "We certainly do not forget you so soon as you forget us. It is, perhaps, our fate rather than our merit. We cannot help ourselves. We live at home, quiet, confined; and our feelings prey upon us. You are forced on exertion." As they continue to debate, Harville says he has never "opened a book in my life which had not something to say upon woman's inconstancy . . . But perhaps you will say, these were all written by men." "Perhaps I shall," says Anne, ". . . I will not allow books to prove anything." This is a subject, she continues, on which we may have opinions but no proof.

I can offer no absolute proof as to how Austen convinces us in this wonderful scene that Anne's and Wentworth's lives hang in the balance, but I hazard the opinion that she practices a kind of synecdoche; the part, romance, stands in for the whole, their social and spiritual beings. Her characters have gone on a pilgrimage and are now able to offer each other nothing but themselves in the best sense of that phrase, which is to say the selves that comprise both their accomplishments and the part of them that will endure even if these accomplishments are stripped away. Together Anne and Wentworth are ready to follow the excellent example of Admiral and Mrs. Croft and face whatever dangers the world holds, by land and sea.

And as readers, we too practice a kind of synecdoche. We put aside the part of ourselves that pretends to want literature to uphold values different from those we have in life, that censures novels for, mostly, not bringing news of war, famine, and revolution. And we accept, even embrace, the delicate and tremulous part of ourselves that yearns for the great good fortune of intimate connection and understanding. I read Austen first as a teenager, then in the company of a long romance, later still as a single woman, and now as a married woman. And in each of these incarnations I have understood that Austen is speaking to me, and about me, and about that deep need we all have to be recognized and to have the world we live in—be it Bath or Baltimore, London or the Lower East Side— make sense.

HUSH, SHUT UP, PLEASE BE QUIET

Letting Our Characters
Tell and Show

I struck the board, and cry'd, No more.
I will abroad.
What? Shall I ever sigh and pine?
My lines and life are free; free as the road,
Loose as the wind, as large as store.
Shall I be still in suit?
Have I no harvest but a thorn
To let me blood, and not restore
What I have lost with cordial fruit?

—GEORGE HERBERT,
"The Collar"

GEORGE HERBERT PUBLISHED "The Collar" in 1633, in a collection called *The Temple*. Nearly four hundred years later it is still impossible to read the poem without hearing the urgency of that first-person voice clamoring at the doors of heaven. We don't have to be religious to enter into the speaker's feeling of being uniquely ill done by, unfairly constrained by a higher power—a deity, a parent, an employer, a partner—and of railing against that power. Along with his slightly older fellow cleric John Donne, author of the equally clamorous "The Sun Rising," Herbert is a superb example of a poet whose quasi-conversational voice speaks to us down the centuries.

Our closest contemporary cousins to these poems are the opinionated, voice-driven narratives of such writers as Sandra Cisneros, Marlon James, Daniel Orozco, Jim Shepherd, and Joy Williams. In their stories, I would suggest, the first-person voice often acts as a substitute for scenes. Someone is talking to us, seizing us by the shoulders, as opposed to calmly narrating a story to the wider world. Such stories tend to have fewer scenes—or sometimes none at all—and we do not miss them. As with Herbert and Donne, urgency carries the day. But setting aside these assertive first-person narrators, most stories and novels require scenes, those moments when events occur more or less in real time and we overhear remarks spoken by, and among, the characters. I would go as far as to say that many of the most revelatory and heartbreaking moments in fiction are played out in scenes. Dialogue is the jewel in the fiction writer's crown, and a jewel ought to shine with particular luster.

By dialogue I do not mean only the actual words spoken by the characters but all the surrounding details that bring those words to life and help to convey their meaning, both overt and covert: where and when the characters are talking, their gestures and expressions, the pauses, the interruptions, and—when we have a close-third or first-person narrator—the thoughts and feelings of the protagonist. Reading the dialogue of playwrights, who use none of these strategies directly, reminds us of how much information is conveyed obliquely in even the most straightforward conversation. Here is Tom Stoppard in an early play, *Every Good Boy Deserves Favour*:

> ALEX: I have a complaint.
>
> DOCTOR (*opening file*): Yes, I know— pathological development of the personality with paranoid delusions.
>
> ALEX: No, there's nothing the matter with me.
>
> DOCTOR (*closing file*): There you are, you see.
>
> ALEX: My complaint is about the man in my cell.
>
> DOCTOR: Ward.
>
> ALEX: He thinks he has an orchestra.
>
> DOCTOR: Yes, he has an identity problem. I forget his name.
>
> ALEX: His behaviour is aggressive.

DOCTOR: He complains about you, too. Apparently you cough during the diminuendos.

ALEX: Is there anything you can do?

DOCTOR: Certainly. (*produces a red pill box from the drawer*) Suck one of these every four hours.

Of course we would get a good deal more out of this conversation from seeing actors perform it. Their intonations and their actions, combined with the set and the lighting, perhaps even sound effects, would all influence how we heard and understood the bare words. And the words are written with that in mind. Stoppard is aspiring to a certain rhythm, a certain tone. Could we take these exchanges verbatim and flesh them out to make a satisfying scene in a story? I suspect not. Even if we were to add in a point of view, gestures, setting, etc., the back-and-forth could easily seem simplistic. The doctor's quip about the patient with an identity problem might come across as trite rather than witty. And the heightened, almost surreal quality of the conversation, with its numerous misunderstandings, would strain credulity in a realistic story.

The same is true in the other direction, turning a story into a play. Even a story with as much dialogue as Hemingway's "Hills Like White Elephants"—so often cited as an example of the dramatic point of view—relies crucially on descriptions of the setting to convey shifts in the characters' thoughts and feelings.

We grow up writing narration, description, and summary in essays and letters, but we seldom have occasion to write dialogue until we turn to fiction. Still, why should it be so hard? Talking is one of our basic human activities; most of us take part in many conversations each day. Aren't these daily exchanges practice for, and a kind of informal research into, the art of dialogue? If the answer were an unequivocal yes, then by the age of twenty-five we would all be writing masterful scenes.

The first and most obvious thing to say is that just as a playwright's dialogue doesn't have the same effect in fiction, neither does a transcription of the exchanges we participate in and overhear. This is particularly surprising when you consider that one of the main things that readers demand of dialogue is that the characters talk in a lifelike or "natural" fashion. But what do they mean by "lifelike"? In our everyday conversations we repeat ourselves, qualify ourselves, fail to finish our sentences, digress, interrupt, start over; we repeatedly fail to use the best possible words in the best possible order. Crises, good or bad, joyful or sorrowful, tend to make us even less eloquent. A transcription of a conversation reveals all of these problems, and more. We would close most books after a few pages if the characters rambled on as we do in daily life. When one stops to look closely at the dialogue in a classic story like, say, Ha Jin's "My Best Soldier," or Flannery O'Connor's "A Good Man Is Hard to Find," one discovers a kind of fictional English that has much more to do with the conventions of fiction than with our normal conversations. Characters, by and large, are succinct, eloquent, witty, intelligent, relevant, and they accomplish all these unnatural things while pretending to speak naturally. Dialogue is a wolf in sheep's clothing—often pretending to be woolly and vague, actually all teeth and meaning. Even characters who are seemingly irrelevant or repetitive are carefully controlled, as Katherine Mansfield demonstrates in this scene from her marvelous story "The Daughters of the Late Colonel." The daughters, Josephine and Constantia, have brought their nephew Cyril to talk to their elderly father:

> "Well," said Grandfather Pinner, beginning to thump, "what have you got to tell me?"
>
> What had he, what had he got to tell him? Cyril felt himself smiling like a perfect imbecile. The room was stifling, too.

But Aunt Josephine came to his rescue. She cried brightly, "Cyril says his father is still very fond of meringues, father dear."

"Eh?" said Grandfather Pinner, curving his hand like a purple meringue shell over one ear.

Josephine repeated, "Cyril says his father is still very fond of meringues."

"Can't hear," said old Colonel Pinner. And he waved Josephine away with his stick, then pointed with his stick to Cyril. "Tell me what she's trying to say," he said.

(My God!) "Must I?" said Cyril. Blushing and staring at Aunt Josephine.

"Do, dear," she smiled. "It will please him so much."

The scene makes perfect use of Colonel Pinner's gestures and of Cyril's thoughts and feelings. Many of the spoken sentences could have been taken from life, but in their concision and in the careful use of repetition, they are far from lifelike. The whole has been crafted into a little comic masterpiece.

Perhaps Mansfield overheard a conversation about meringues. Certainly, for most fiction writers, eavesdropping is an essential vice. One day last year I arrived in class to find my students discussing how, and whether, to whiten one's teeth. I scribbled down their conversation; this was just what I needed for one of my characters. But while eavesdropping can be very helpful—we catch a line here, a phrase there—most extended dialogue in fiction cannot, as I already remarked, be taken directly from life. It resembles more closely what we wish we'd said rather than what we actually do say. The French have an expression: *la pensée d'escalier*—literally "the thought on the stairs"—which means those brilliant retorts that come to us only as we descend the stairs after leaving a dinner party. Our characters are the ones who get to utter these belated thoughts.

How we write dialogue is partly a matter of convention; so too is how we read it. Both readers and writers, for instance, have come to accept that a first-person narrator can tell a story in a very different voice from that in which she or he addresses other characters. In James Joyce's "Araby," for example, we have a very eloquent narrator. "North Richmond Street, being blind," he tells us, "was a quiet street except at the hour when the Christian Brothers' School set the boys free. An uninhabited house of two stories stood at the blind end, detached from its neighbors in a square ground." But when he finally speaks to the girl he's interested in, he can only stammer out a few phrases. The narrators of Raymond

Carver's "Cathedral" and ZZ Packer's "Drinking Coffee Elsewhere" are in the same tradition: very articulate when talking to us; surly and often tongue-tied when talking to anyone else. That readers willingly accept this apparent contradiction demonstrates, I think, not only the power of convention in fiction but also the degree to which we all suffer from *la pensée d'escalier*. We know from intimate experience that someone who can barely string two words together can have an eloquent inner voice. Authors, knowing this, typically do not bother to explain the gap between narration and conversation; they trust the reader to understand. But there are first-person narratives in which there is almost no gap. Huck Finn addresses the reader and his fellow characters in the same rich combination of vernacular and dialect. More recently, in *Paddy Clarke Ha Ha Ha* the Irish writer Roddy Doyle achieves a striking effect by having ten-year-old Paddy narrate and talk in almost the same voice:

> I did my eccer in braille. It took ages, being careful not to rip the page with the needle. There were all little dots on the kitchen table when I was finished. I showed the braille to my da.
> —What's this?
> —Braille. Blind people's writing.

He closed his eyes and felt the bumps on the page.

—What does it say? he asked.

—It's my English homework, I told him.—Fifteen lines about your favourite pet.

—Is the teacher blind?

—No. I was just doing it. I did it properly as well.

Doyle risks Paddy coming across as simplistic, even childish, by largely ignoring the convention that would allow him to talk like a ten-year-old and narrate like a thirty-five-year-old. The result is an apparently artless novel that is entirely artful.

Another requirement of the natural-seeming quality is that dialogue should not sound expository, unless overexplaining is clearly a character trait. We do not want characters saying, "Darling, now that our children despite numerous setbacks are safely at university and you've been promoted to deputy manager of a small suburban shop, it's time to finally visit Ontario and see the house where Alice Munro lives." Such speeches make us feel that the author is putting words into the mouths of the characters, using them to give essential information, rather than letting them speak for themselves. Which is not to say that a character cannot convincingly announce an obvious fact: "Mum, I'm eighteen." "Richard, you're always late."

But if all dialogue does is appear natural, then its artifice is wasted. Good dialogue serves the story. It must reveal the characters in ways that the narration cannot and advance the plot while, ideally, not appearing too flagrant in either mission. And it must deepen the psychic life of the story. We should sense the tectonic plates shifting beneath the spoken words. There is text, and there is subtext. Too much dialogue without subtext can quickly become tedious.

Beyond all that dialogue can accomplish in terms of characterization and plot, its mere presence on the page creates space and energy. Readers of fiction sometimes get discouraged when faced with dense paragraph after dense paragraph. Rereading *One Hundred Years of Solitude*, I was struck by what short shrift Gabriel García Márquez gives dialogue. Many of his paragraphs are longer than a page; most of his scenes are less than fifteen lines. He tells and tells and tells and such dialogue as does occur is often embedded in a paragraph. In less masterful hands this could easily overwhelm the reader, but, such is the amazing fertility of García Márquez's imagination and the luster of his prose, that we read raptly. What will happen next to the town of Macondo and the Buendía family?

Very few novels, however, can get away with this much telling. But very few can be told entirely in scenes. When people in workshops shout, "Show don't tell," they are clamoring for the energy that dialogue brings, but that energy comes in part from the contrast between telling and showing. In any story with more than one scene a rhythm gradually emerges as the prose alternates between scene and narration, a rhythm that the author will often break or disrupt at the crucial moment. In "The Daughters of the Late Colonel," Mansfield goes back and forth between scene and narration until the last pages of the story, when, to devastating effect, she gives the crucial exposition: how the daughters' early loss of their mother, combined with their narrow social circle, has limited their lives; how there never were any men to marry. We know, as we read the last paragraphs, that Constantia and Josephine will only ever be daughters and sisters.

The choice of when to give the exposition, the background story, is often a complicated one. (In *The Great Gatsby* Fitzgerald kept trying to find a place to reveal Gatsby's past, finally settling on chapter seven.) Most authors are also choosing on almost every page whether to present material dramatically, in a scene, or in narration. There are no rules for how to make these decisions—we make them story by story, chapter by chapter—but consider the following. I can write a scene in which Lucy and Tabitha are walking through the woods, trying to find a vernal pond:

> "You copied my chemistry homework," said Lucy, nonchalantly.
>
> "No, I didn't." Tabitha stabbed a clump of grass with her stick. "Anyway what makes you think you're Marie Curie?"
>
> "I'm not interested in being Curie. All that mud. I want to be Alexander Fleming. He was Scottish and he discovered penicillin. Do you think we should whiten our teeth this summer?"

Or I can write:

> Walking in the woods, searching for the vernal pond, Lucy and Tabitha bickered about whether they wished they'd discovered radium or penicillin.

Which is better depends on which story I am trying to tell. Scenes slow time down; narration speeds it up. Some writers generate their material only through writing scenes; they might need to compose two pages of the girls bickering in order to craft one elegant sentence of summary. Sometimes only in revision, as we begin to grasp the larger meaning of the work, can we decide what should be compressed into narration and what should be expanded into scene.

And, as in other areas of life, size makes a difference. One way we direct our readers' attention is by how we use the space of the story. Showing Lucy and Tabitha arguing for two pages suggests that something more is at stake than copying homework, and that we are learning something new about the characters—why else go on at such length? Which is not to say that bigger is necessarily better. Sometimes, to paraphrase Isaac Babel, one piercing sentence can nail the reader's heart more effectively than a scene of several pages.

So while we may go back and forth in various drafts, moving material into scene or into narration, the two are not interchangeable. Narration compresses information. Dialogue can allow us to convey information—emotional or psychological—of which neither the characters nor the narrator is fully aware. Dialogue is not only showing as opposed to telling, it is also showing what cannot be told. In "The Daughters of the Late Colonel" Mansfield shows, in scene after scene, the childlike nature of the two sisters; only gradually do we learn that they are in their forties. At no point does she summarize or diagnose them. The reader comes to empathize with Constantia and Josephine in a way that no one around them does.

But if dialogue typically can be strengthened by details of setting, gestures, and various interruptions, these can also be a liability:

> "Would you like some salad?" Richard asked Veronica. He had grown up with iceberg lettuce that looked as if it had never seen the sun and only as an adult discovered the many possibilities of leafy vegetables. His current favorite was rocket, bitter and peppery with a zigzaggy leaf that made you want to add your own tooth marks but if you had asked him last spring he would have ardently defended radicchio, which his mother claimed had been discovered by a gardener at the Vatican . . .

Properly handled, this kind of digression can be illuminating and pleasurable. But if done at too great length, or too frequently, it runs the risk that we will have forgotten all about Richard's not very interesting question before Veronica answers. Or such is usually the case. In Nicholson Baker's short novel *The Mezzanine* the narrator's digressions and ruminations, as he makes his way from the lobby to the mezzanine, become the novel.

At the other extreme we have the kind of dialogue that resembles a volley at Wimbledon: a page of one- or two-line exchanges with almost no stage directions, attributions, or interruptions:

> "What were you doing to the dog?" John said.
>
> > "Nothing," said Lena.
> >
> > "I saw you tug his ears."
> >
> > "There was a leaf caught in his fur."
> >
> > "What kind of leaf?"
> >
> > "What do you mean 'what kind of leaf?'
> A brown leaf. A dead leaf. Who cares?"
> >
> > "The vet said Alfie was in perfect health."
> >
> > "Until he dropped dead in a ditch. Is that your definition of perfect health?"

This kind of dialogue moves very quickly. George Higgins uses it to masterful effect in his classic thriller *The Friends of Eddie Coyle.* The risk with these volleys, however, is that readers may miss the shifts in meaning and the subtext. The pauses, the spaces between speeches, slow a scene down in a way that enables us to grasp what is happening at a deeper level, to follow the emotional swerves of the characters. In stories written in the first person or the close third, these pauses often include the narrator's thoughts. Here are Elliot and his wife, Grace, in Robert Stone's story "Helping":

> She came into the kitchen and sat down at the table to take off her boots. Her lean, freckled face was flushed with the cold, but her eyes looked weary. "I wish you'd put those skis down in the barn," she told him. "You never use them."
>
> "I always like to think," Elliot said, "that I'll start the morning off skiing."
>
> "Well, you never do," she said. "How long have you been home?"
>
> "Practically just walked in," he said. Her pointing out that he no longer skied in the morning enraged him. "I stopped at the Conway Library to get the new Oxford *Classical World.* Candace ordered it."
>
> Her look grew troubled. She had caught something in his voice. With dread and bitter satisfaction, Elliot watched his wife detect the smell of whiskey.
>
> "Oh, God," she said. "I don't believe it."

> Let's get it over with, he thought. Let's
> have the song and dance.

Note how Stone uses Elliot's thoughts to let us know the chasm between what he says—"I stopped at the Conway Library"—and what he feels—"enraged." And in the last few lines the description of Elliot's feelings also allows Grace to detect the smell of whiskey.

This is a good moment to point out that another way in which dialogue can seem unnatural, or expository, is when a character reveals too much. I admit I am biased on this topic. I come from a culture that believes that talking about one's feelings is bad form— my father, after nearly dying of pneumonia one Christmas, wrote to me that he had been a little under the weather—but in daily life people are often reluctant to reveal their deepest feelings for all kinds of reasons: shame, timidity, fear of not being heard, fear of being heard. In Elliot's exchange with Grace, what husband and wife don't say, or can't say, or won't say, is a powerful aspect of what is being communicated.

❁

Part of the pleasure of George Herbert's "The Collar" is the colloquial passion with which the narrator addresses his deity. In writing dialogue we are always choosing not just what our characters say, but how they say it. Hush. Please be quiet. Shut the hell up. Keep it down. Silence. Put a sock in it. May I kindly have your attention.

Each of these remarks conveys the same basic information but conveys it in a distinct way. Clearly the speakers and/or the situations are different—a woman might say hush to her child and shut the hell up to her husband—and the connotations vary. We'd be surprised, perhaps pleasantly, if a Denis Johnson character said, "Hush," or if one of Alice Munro's country widows said, "Put a sock in it." As we start to write dialogue we establish the level of diction for each character. Is a character going to use high diction, or low, or some mixture of the two? Is an eight-year-old going to say "preposterous"? In my novel *Criminals* I had a private rule that no two characters could use the same swear words.

And here we often find ourselves caught between the Scylla and Charybdis of wanting to create strong, original characters and worrying about the reader's expectations. We make our character say something interesting and insightful and suddenly the reader is insisting that a supermarket cashier in Chattanooga would never use the word "authenticate," or that a Maine fisherman would never quote Wordsworth's "Intimations of

Immortality." The writer is trying to transcend stereotypes; the reader is clinging to them. One of the barriers to writing sparkling, inventive dialogue is that unhelpful workshop response: she/he would never say that. The workshop may well be right, but it is worth fighting for our characters' best lines. Before settling for more pedestrian dialogue, we can try to deepen our characters. Yes, most fishermen don't care for the Romantic poets, but this one does. His great-aunt took him on a tour of the Lake District when he was twelve.

I mentioned the rhythm created by alternating between scene and narration, but dialogue also has an internal rhythm. Many writers write scenes of almost the same length, in almost the same way, irrespective of the story, the situation, or the particular characters. Everyone makes two-line speeches or four-line speeches, or whatever that author's favorite unit of speech may be. The same goes for the attributions, interruptions, and gestures. Everyone answers, or pauses, or folds their arms. A crucial respect in which we can improve our dialogue is by figuring out our particular pattern and seeing whether we can usefully alter, or expand, it. We would not want all characters to speak at such robust length as Philip Roth's do in *The Human Stain*—many of the speeches are a dozen lines or more—but it is good to know that our characters could hold forth if the need arose. Or, alternatively, be succinct.

Another of my private rules for writing dialogue, one I stole from Ford Maddox Ford, is that characters should not always answer each other, or should answer in unexpected ways:

> "Your petunias are looking grand, Mrs. Ashton," I said, waving my umbrella toward her exuberant window boxes.
>
> "I notice your granddaughter hasn't stopped in this month," she said. "Nor last either."

Following this rule too strictly can lead to exasperatingly surreal exchanges, but in real life people often fail to respond directly to questions and comments. Having characters answer each other too precisely can become predictable and expository. Which in turn deadens a scene.

✿

So far I have been describing dialogue in which the spoken words are reported verbatim, but an essential, and very useful, kind of dialogue is indirect speech. There are many occasions when the reader should not be subjected to every word a character utters. *Julia began to explain rocket science. James launched into an account of his nephew's performance in the school play.* Indirect speech allows the writer to summarize in a powerful fashion that still suggests the spoken words. The choice between quoting and summarizing is not necessarily a binary one:

> My mother never had a good word to say about nature. On the balmiest of May evenings, after a long, hard winter, when the five of us gathered on the bridge to watch my brother fish, she would remark that she had heard that buttercups emit a dangerous gas. "And lilacs," she went on, warming to her subject, "can be fatal to people who are lactose intolerant."

Here I'm combining indirect speech—we don't want to hear the mother talk at length—with a brief glimpse of her conversation.

Which brings me to what I call the "mini-scene": a moment of dialogue, or a quotation, in the middle of a narrative passage. Alice Munro and William Trevor are both masters of this. Here, for example, is Trevor in his great story "The Ballroom of Romance":

> But on Saturday nights Bridie forgot the scotch grass and the soil. In different dresses she cycled to the dance-hall, encouraged to make the journey by her father. "Doesn't it do you good, girl," he'd say, as though he imagined she begrudged herself the pleasure. "Why wouldn't you enjoy yourself?" She'd cook him his tea and then he'd settle down with the wireless, or maybe a Wild West novel.

The father's actual words—his warmth and good humor—give us a much more vivid sense of his character, and of his relationship with Bridie, than if we simply read that he encouraged her.

❋

Manners, good and bad, play a crucial part in dialogue. An editor of one of my early novels complained that all my characters—nice British people—kept offering each other cups of tea. In daily life politeness is a virtue. We want people to ask after each other's health, to say please and thank you, to comment on the weather. But on the page politeness can quickly become boring. Rudeness, or at the very least terseness, is sometimes essential. Let good manners be implied. Once it is established that a character is mannerly you don't need to show that in every exchange. On the other hand, a rude character suddenly being polite, or a polite character lapsing into rudeness, can be very interesting.

Telephone manners represent a special challenge for the contemporary writer. Conversations, in life and in fiction, frequently occur on the phone, and we can (usually) see only one character:

> Wilfred counted to the third ring and then picked up his phone. "Hello," he said.
>
> "Hello," said a woman's voice. "It's Vanessa."
>
> "Vanessa. I haven't heard from you in ages. How are you?"
>
> "I'm all right. I had a cold last week but I'm better now. How are you?"
>
> "I'm great. Really good. Thank you. What's up?"
>
> "Not a lot. I just thought I'd call. I saw Madeleine last night."

Without a sense of subtext, this quickly grows tedious, and several such conversations, with the ritual exchanges of identity and greetings, can bring a story to a standstill. Once again, I would argue that rudeness, or implied politeness, has its place. Just as we often omit the humdrum details of our characters' journeys, so too we can omit the preliminaries that pave the way to the substance of their conversations.

❉

There is one last aspect of dialogue that I want to address. In my opening paragraphs I offered the traditional claim that readers respond to dialogue because it is a chance to hear the characters speak for themselves. I think this is true, but I also think that, over and above all the requirements of character and story, dialogue, in some ineffable way, is deeply rooted in the author's narrative voice. This is one of the several reasons why it is hard to imagine transposing even a single line of dialogue from, say, Elizabeth Bowen to Graham Greene, or from Julia Alvarez to Junot Díaz.

What this relationship between narrative voice and dialogue is, and how it works, is something I have seldom seen discussed, and most of the writers with whom I have broached the topic seem unaware of the degree to which their voices inform those of their characters. Certainly most readers are oblivious to this secret connection and notice it only in the case of such extreme examples as, say, Hemingway's "A Clean Well-Lighted Place," Richard Brautigan's "1/3, 1/3, 1/3," or Grace Paley's "Faith in a Tree." But if you line up pages of scene and narration by half a dozen of your favorite writers I think you'll begin to see how the two are linked. Deborah Eisenberg's "Some Other, Better Otto" is a wonderful example of an unusually graceful connection between dialogue and narrative voice:

> Who was too good for whom? It often came down to a show of force. When Corinne had called a week or so earlier about Thanksgiving, Otto, addled by alarm, said, "We're having people ourselves, I'm afraid."
>
> Corinne's silence was like a mirror, flashing his tiny, harmless lie back to him in huge magnification, all covered with sticky hairs and microbes.
>
> "Well, I'll see what I can do," he said.
>
> "Please try," Corinne said. The phrase had the unassailable authority of a road sign appearing suddenly around the bend: FALLING ROCK. "Otto, the children are growing up."

As with Elliot in "Helping," the discrepancy between what Otto thinks and feels and what he actually says to his sister makes these ordinary remarks glitter with meaning and becomes part of both the plot and the theme of the story. Meanwhile the wit of the close-third person prepares us for the eloquence that Otto demonstrates in other conversations. The story as a whole reveals not just Otto's but also Eisenberg's unique sensibility.

Perhaps this relationship between dialogue and narrative voice is so intimate, so particular to each writer, that it cannot be examined as an element of craft. Perhaps we should take refuge in Keats's Negative Capability—that desirable state of mind that allows a person to embrace "uncertainties, Mysteries, doubts, without any irritable reaching after fact & reason"— and let the rest be silence. But for all my Scottish reticence, I think there is a little further to go. Marilynne Robinson offers some guidance in this complicated terrain. In her teaching and her conversation, Robinson often refers to the question of consciousness for characters, narrators, and authors. My intuition is that the secret connection between dialogue and narration has to do with making our work more fully conscious, and with inhabiting that consciousness at the deepest level. One of the triumphs of Hilary Mantel's recent novel *Wolf Hall* is her ability to suggest, in both dialogue and narration, how people thought and spoke in the sixteenth century. The two voices work together to reveal a single consciousness.

So yes, our characters do speak for themselves, they do have lives of their own, but those lives are lived in the worlds we create, past, present, and future. Our task as fiction writers is to hone our voices, both in narration and dialogue, so that our characters speak more truly as themselves and, at the same time, speak more truly as inhabitants of those worlds.

EVEN ONE DAY

Considering Aesthetics
with Virginia Woolf

*She always had the feeling that it was very, very
dangerous to live even one day.*

—Mrs Dalloway

SEVENTY-FIVE YEARS AFTER her death in 1941, Virginia Woolf remains, as she was in her lifetime, a household name among writers and readers. She has one of the all-time best author photographs, the title of a famous play (and film) contains her name, *A Room of One's Own* is part of the feminist canon, and she is revered as a great modernist novelist; indeed she is among the handful of writers who helped to invent modernism. All of this might make us forget that for thirty years after her death she was seen as a marginal figure and that even now, I would suggest, her name—outside of college classrooms—is mentioned more often than her pages are read. *To the Lighthouse* is widely regarded as her most significant novel and remains a stubborn, radiant, difficult, and truthful book, one that repays our attention and one to which many writers, know it or not, like it or not, are indebted.

As in much of Woolf's most enduring work, *To the Lighthouse* combines deeply autobiographical material with a clear aesthetic agenda. She is—it cannot be said too often—among our foremost stylists; her sentences and paragraphs have much to teach all practicing writers. But it is from examining the way in which she explains her aesthetic principles and then uses them to shape her material that we can learn the most. Every writer has a set of aesthetic beliefs—even if they're not fully articulated—but very seldom do I hear myself, or my friends, cite these beliefs to defend or explain our work. Most of us, I suspect, have not taken the trouble to figure out what we are writing against. Or what we are writing toward. We are working, mostly in the tradition of realism. Does anything more need to be said? I would argue the answer is yes. We have much to gain from figuring out, as Woolf did in her letters, essays, and reviews, what our beliefs are and how we can embody them in our fictions.

Perhaps the word "aesthetic" has a daunting ring, so let me suggest a more pragmatic approach. Let us follow Woolf's example and ask ourselves four questions:

1. Which writers, past or present, can teach us the most and give us the best tools for our own work?

2. What makes characters real for us as readers, and how, as writers, can we create such characters in our work?

3. What is new in the world that we need to capture in our novels and stories?

4. How can the answers to these first three questions help us to shape our intimate material in a way that avoids the dangers of mere autobiography?

Woolf spent much of her writing life asking, and answering, these questions. Her journey to the lighthouse required her to resolve various intellectual challenges as well as her relationship to her family history. No wonder ten years have to pass before Mr. Ramsay, at the end of the novel, finally jumps ashore.

✿

Virginia was born in 1882 into what she described as "a very communicative, literate, letter writing, visiting, articulate, late-nineteenth-century world." Her father, Sir Leslie Stephen, was a writer and literary critic. The year she was born he embarked on the *Dictionary of National Biography*, which, in 1902, would earn him a knighthood. Her mother, Julia Duckworth, was a famous beauty (when that seems to have been a full-time job) and was related to the famous photographer Julia Cameron. Julia and Leslie began their marriage with two children apiece—each had already been married and widowed—and had four more of their own, of whom Virginia was the third. In their busy household, Virginia later wrote, she could hardly remember ever being alone with her mother.

Her childhood was divided between their large London house and the house they leased in Cornwall. Every summer, the entire family moved down to the seaside town of St. Ives for several months. This annual migration ended abruptly with Julia's death in May 1895, when Virginia was thirteen. The idyllic house, with the sea nearby and the lighthouse in the distance, became even more idyllic by virtue of being forever lost. Leslie, widowed for a second time, mourned his wife with desperate tyranny. No one else was allowed to mourn her; no one else was mourning her sufficiently. Virginia learned early to scrutinize her emotions—and often to find them wanting. Her half-sister, Stella, took over the running of the household, but in 1897, only a few months after her marriage, she, too, died suddenly. "We never spoke of them," Virginia wrote. "I can remember how awkwardly Thoby avoided saying 'Stella' when a ship called *Stella* was wrecked." (Thoby, her older brother, died of typhoid in 1906.)

While her brothers attended school and went on to Cambridge University, Virginia and her older sister, Vanessa (later the painter Vanessa Bell), were educated at home and given the run of their father's library. Although Virginia famously wrote in her diary that if her father hadn't died, there would have been no novels, no work, he nevertheless took his daughters seriously and gave them unusual intellectual freedom. After he died from cancer in 1904, the four siblings moved into a house in the neighborhood of London known as Bloomsbury. Henry James, a long-time acquaintance of the family, was particularly appalled by their Bohemian lifestyle. Virginia began to publish reviews, and Thoby and Adrian, her younger brother, brought their university friends home to visit. Among these young men was Leonard Woolf, whom Virginia married in 1912—the same year in which the *Titanic* sank, Captain Scott reached the South Pole, and Thomas Mann published *Death in Venice.*

The year after her marriage, Virginia finished her first novel, *The Voyage Out*, and had a nervous breakdown, her third, during which she made a suicide attempt, her second. Hermione Lee, to whose wonderful biography I am indebted throughout this essay, writes that Leonard made Virginia's illness one of his life's works. "He documents her illness," Lee writes, "with the same scrupulous integrity, exhaustiveness and attempt at objectivity that he would apply to the minutes of the Labour Party's Advisory Committee on International Relations." He tried to keep Virginia from becoming overly stimulated, or overly tired, both of which sometimes led to the episodes of madness (her word) that she experienced throughout her life. It was his decision that they should not have children. On March 28, 1941, driven to despair by the voices in her head, Virginia walked into the River Ouse with stones in her pockets. She was fifty-nine years old. Leonard survived her by more than twenty-five years. In 1965, he went to see Edward Albee's play—he had given permission for the title—and noted how moved he was by George and Martha and the theme of childlessness. With admirable if infuriating discretion, he never divulged exactly how he and Virginia had negotiated this question, or many others, during their long marriage.

❁

I mention these details not to pathologize one of our most productive writers, but because Woolf's relationship with her own consciousness, her acute awareness of moments of being, and her struggle to find a language with which to convey those moments, along with her mental and physical states, lies at the heart of her aesthetics and informs all her mature work. Here she is writing in her diary in 1937, shortly before the publication of *The Years*:

> I wish I could write out my sensations at this moment. They are so peculiar & so unpleasant. . . . A physical feeling as if I were drumming slightly in the veins: very cold: impotent: & terrified. As if I were exposed on a high ledge in full light. Very lonely. L. out to lunch. Nessa has Quentin & don't want me. Very useless. No atmosphere round me. No words. Very apprehensive. As if something cold & horrible—a roar of laughter at my expense were about to happen. And I am powerless to ward it off: I have no protection.

According to her nephew Quentin Bell, she could not bear to record her mental state during her breakdowns; what she mostly spoke of were the physical symptoms—the drumming, the cold, the lack of atmosphere—that accompanied her illnesses.

Despite Woolf's ill health during the first years of their marriage, she and Leonard became companions and helpmates, sharing work and a wide social circle. By the time she published *To the Lighthouse* in 1927, she was forty-five and had, as she herself acknowledged, more freedom than any other writer in England. This was due not so much to her fame, although she was becoming better known every year, but to her work being published by the Hogarth Press, which she and Leonard had started in 1917 and ran together. If Leonard approved—and he did—then the work was published. In 1922 he thought *Jacob's Room* her best work, a work of genius. In 1925 he thought *Mrs Dalloway* her best. In 1927 we find Woolf writing in her diary, "Well Leonard has read *To the Lighthouse*, and says it is much my best book, & it is a 'masterpiece.' . . . He calls it entirely new 'a psychological poem,' is his name for it.'" It's hard not to wish that every writer could have her own Leonard.

Woolf not only had unusual freedom as a writer; she was also unusually prolific in four genres. As a fiction writer, she wrote novels and stories. As a critic, she wrote close to five hundred reviews, essays, and lectures. She kept a diary, which she was always railing against—why am I writing here again? she asks repeatedly. And she wrote many, many letters. All of this material has contributed to her reputation, and gives us a remarkable degree of insight into her methods as a writer. Moreover, through the Hogarth Press, through her friendships and her reviewing, she was deeply involved with other writers and acutely aware of what was going on in literature and art. Despite her productivity, her early work was not particularly precocious. It was not until she was nearly forty, working on *Jacob's Room* in the aftermath of the First World War, that she felt she had begun at last to find her voice, her vision.

In her famous essay "Mr. Bennett and Mrs. Brown," written in 1924, the year before *Mrs Dalloway* was published, Woolf offers a strong argument for her aesthetics. In doing so she describes three groups of writers: the Victorians, whom she by and large admires; her immediate predecessors the Edwardians—Mr. Bennett, Mr. Galsworthy, and H. G. Wells—whom she by and large deplores; and herself and her peers, whom she calls the Georgians, and whom we now call the modernists. Among these last Woolf numbers E. M. Forster, D. H. Lawrence, Lytton Strachey, James Joyce (the Hogarth Press rejected *Ulysses* because it was too long), and T. S. Eliot (whom the press briefly published before he took his work elsewhere). The list includes no women but, by implication, Woolf includes herself, Katherine Mansfield, and Elizabeth Bowen. At the end of "Mr. Bennett and Mrs. Brown," she writes, "I will make one final and surpassingly rash prediction—we are trembling on the verge of one of the great ages of English literature." In fact, by 1924 there was nothing rash about the prediction. The great age was fully present.

Like *A Room of One's Own*, "Mr. Bennett and Mrs. Brown" began as a talk, and like that iconic work it retains the freshness of Woolf's speaking voice. She begins by making two assertions: Everyone in this room is a judge of character and, more debatable, "in or about December, 1910, human character changed." Halley's comet appeared in 1910, Tolstoy died, and Edward VII was succeeded by George V, but the specific date is commonly taken to refer to the exhibition of impressionist paintings organized by Woolf's friend, the painter and critic Roger Fry. Impressionism has become so familiar, almost a cliché, that it's hard to remember how revolutionary it was to think of art as not being representational. A rose was a rose was a rose. Now, suddenly, the subjective—who saw the rose, how they saw it—was as important, sometimes even more important, than the actual flower. In *To the Lighthouse*, when the painter Lily Briscoe asks what Mr. Ramsay's work is about, his son Andrew says, "'Subject and object and the nature of reality,' . . . And when she [Lily] said Heavens, she had no notion what that meant. 'Think of a kitchen table then,' he told her, 'when you're not there.'"

At the heart of "Mr. Bennett and Mrs. Brown" is an argument about character: what it is and how, at the deepest and most truthful level, it can be conjured onto the page. Woolf's main objection to the Edwardians, who she is writing against, is their obfuscating didacticism, which she claims conceals rather than reveals character. She and her colleagues are the new realists, the writers who are trying to portray the shifts in human nature and in the contemporary world. Only a few years later, the German physicist Werner Heisenberg published what became known as the uncertainty principle, but Woolf was already well aware that uncertainty would be the ruling principle of her century. Near the end of *To the Lighthouse*, one of the characters thinks, "Nothing was simply one thing"—a sentence that could stand as a motto for both the life of this complicated writer and the experience of reading her fiction.

Woolf returns over and over in her work to two pressing questions: how to capture the simultaneity of experience and, increasingly as she grows older, how to capture the sensibility of women. She herself worries that no one likes her hat and that no one likes her novels. Can she include both kinds of worry in her work? This is the writer who refers to having her hair "bingled"—i.e., cut short—as one of the great events of her life; from behind, she says, she looks like a partridge's rear. She is also the writer who claims that women have to invent a new syntax and yet must write androgynously. She hoped *Mrs Dalloway* was a masterpiece and was thrilled that it earned enough money for the Woolfs to have an indoor toilet installed at their country home (she and Leonard enjoyed showing guests how well it flushed).

On May 14, 1925, the day *Mrs Dalloway* was published, she wrote in her diary about her idea for a new novel:

> This is going to be fairly short: to have father's character done complete in it; & mother's; & St Ives; & childhood; & all the usual things I try to put in—life, death, &c. But the centre is father's character, sitting in a boat, reciting We perished, each alone, while he crushes a dying mackerel—However, I must refrain. I must write a few little stories first, & let the Lighthouse simmer, adding to it between tea & dinner till it is complete for writing out.

Later she would tell Vanessa that *To the Lighthouse* had come to her all at once, in a great rush, as she walked round Tavistock Square near her home in London.

Note that word "complete," used twice in the above paragraph and an important term in Woolf's aesthetic vocabulary. For her, a good novel is a complete novel; we can hold it whole in our minds and when we get to the end of it all we want to do is reread it, to understand it more deeply. As examples she gives Laurence Sterne's *Tristram Shandy* and the work of Jane Austen. When you think of a great novel, she claims, you think of "some character who seemed to you so real" and then you think of all the things you think of through that character's eyes—"of religion, of love, of war, of peace, of family life, of balls in country towns, of sunsets, moonrises, the immortality of the soul." The job of the novelist, she contends, is to show us character and the world through character.

For the next few months, after having her rush of ideas, Woolf gathered ingredients for the novel, waiting for it to "simmer," to "thicken." "The sea," she writes, "is to be heard all through it." She was worried that the theme might be sentimental—to her one of the great vices and a charge one reviewer had brought against *Mrs Dalloway*. And she pondered whether *To the Lighthouse* would really be a novel or should it be called something else—perhaps an elegy?

By August 1925, she knew that the novel would be in three parts—part one would have "a sense of waiting, of expectation: the child waiting to go to the lighthouse: the woman awaiting the return of the couple." Joining parts one and three would be "an interesting experiment . . . giving the sense of ten years passing." She also records that the emphasis has now shifted from Mr. Ramsay to Mrs. Ramsay and includes a little sketch of the new work: "Two blocks joined by a corridor." The corridor, the middle part where ten years pass, was going to contain all the lyrical passages she wanted to write so that they wouldn't interrupt the narrative elsewhere.

Woolf's planning of the novel fills me with admiration. Like many writers I know, I do not (so far) outline my work in advance. I begin a novel with a destination in mind but the route is vague. Any attempt to map the journey will, I worry, render the unwritten pages artificial and ridiculous. But Woolf is fearless in setting up goals and markers for herself. I wonder if she knew of Henry James's notebooks, in which he famously worked out the plots of several of his great novels, going back to them in entry after entry until the psychological arc of the novel was finally clear.

One more thing we need to keep in mind as we approach *To the Lighthouse* is Woolf's objections to the Edwardians. They want, she claims, something from their reader; their books are incomplete and they force us to go outside the book. "I believe," she writes in "Mr. Bennett and Mrs. Brown," "that all novels . . . Deal with character, and that it is to express character—not to preach doctrines, sing songs, or celebrate the glories of the British Empire, that the form of the novel, so clumsy, verbose and undramatic, so rich, elastic and alive, has been evolved." Much of the essay describes a short train journey from Richmond to London and Woolf's observations of two of her fellow passengers: a woman in her sixties, whom she calls Mrs. Brown, and a man in his forties, whom she calls Mr. Smith. From the details of their appearance and the exchanges she overhears, she invents a rich inner life and a dramatic history. On first reading the essay I assumed that much of this was fictionalized later, but the writer Nigel Nicholson gives a vivid account of Woolf entertaining him as a small boy by making up stories about the strangers they met.

To the Lighthouse surely does strike some readers as "clumsy, verbose and undramatic." As an early reviewer remarked, it is a novel in which nothing and everything happens. Each of the three parts is narrated in the third person, in short numbered sections—some only a few lines long, some a dozen pages—and each takes place in the same location, a large house by the sea. Woolf describes the house as being on the Hebrides in Scotland but makes almost no effort to disguise her beloved Cornwall.

Part one, "The Window," follows one evening in the lives of Mr. and Mrs. Ramsay, their eight children, their guests, and their, for the most part, conveniently invisible servants. The point of view moves fluently among the various characters and an omniscient narrator. The reader, especially in the opening sections, must sit at attention as Woolf ignores the normal boundaries and gathers facts, thoughts, and sensations, past and present, into long, sinuous sentences. Yes, if it's fine, Mrs. Ramsay tells her son James, they can go to the lighthouse tomorrow.

In the hundred and twenty pages that follow, Mr. and Mrs. Ramsay argue and are reconciled. We are shown Mr. Ramsay's doubts: Is he a genius? In the alphabet of knowledge will he ever get past *Q*? Will his books last? All the questions Woolf asked herself. We are shown through the various guests Mrs. Ramsay's beauty and her insight into her husband's frailty. Meanwhile, in the garden, Lily Briscoe, a single woman in her thirties, struggles to paint a picture of the house. The zenith of the evening is a wonderfully Proustian dinner of *boeuf en daube.* At first the meal seems headed for disaster. "Nothing seemed to have merged," Mrs. Ramsay thinks. "They all sat separate." But with the help of Lily, the candlelight, and the delicious food, she at last brings everyone together. Just for a moment the chaos of life is averted and everyone is caught in a golden net, merged and complete. This kind of unity is what Lily's painting promises and what Mr. Ramsay is seeking as he strives to get past *Q.* Woolf described the scene as one of the best things she'd ever written, a triumph of her method.

Part two, "Time Passes"—the corridor—begins the same evening with the characters heading to bed. Woolf purposefully echoes Lord Grey's famous remark on the eve of the First World War: "The lamps are going out all over Europe; we shall not see them lit again in our lifetime." The sixteen pages that follow cover ten years, during which Mrs. Ramsay dies, as well as two of the children. The deaths are dealt with briefly; they are, literally, in parentheses. "(Mr. Ramsay, stumbling along a passage one dark morning, stretched his arms out, but Mrs. Ramsay having died rather suddenly the night before, his arms, though stretched out, remained empty.)" It's hard not to recall Woolf's comment about her dead siblings: "We never spoke of them."

Most of "Time Passes" is devoted to the house, which, for nearly a decade, is almost overwhelmed by wind and weather and is finally rescued when the family announces their return. Woolf wrote this section during the general strike of 1926, and she noted how the darkness and confusion of the strike had crept into her work: the women who rescue the house can be read as representatives of the stoic working people.

Part three, "The Lighthouse," like "The Window," takes place within a few hours. The long delayed voyage occurs. The narrative alternates between Mr. Ramsay in the boat with two of his children, sailing toward the lighthouse, and Lily Briscoe in the garden, once again struggling to paint the house. As she paints, Lily thinks about Mrs. Ramsay, who, in death, looms almost as large as she had in life. "Think about a table when you're not there." Or when it's not there. The descriptions of Mrs. Ramsay are informed both by Woolf's memories of her mother and by her affair with the writer Vita Sackville-West, which was, during the months she wrote this section, at its most ardent.

The novel ends with Mr. Ramsay arriving at the lighthouse and Lily finishing her picture. "With a sudden intensity, as if she saw it clear for a second, she drew a line there, in the centre. It was done; it was finished. Yes, she thought, laying down her brush in extreme fatigue, I have had my vision." The last sentence of the novel, like the first, begins with the word "yes."

In "Mr. Bennett and Mrs. Brown," Woolf takes the Edwardians to task for their approach to creating character. "I asked them—they are my elders and betters—How shall I begin to describe this woman's character? And they said: 'Begin by saying that her father kept a shop in Harrogate. Ascertain the rent. Ascertain the wages of the shop assistants in the year 1878. Discover what her mother died of. Describe cancer. Describe calico. Describe—'" She goes on to explain the tremendous efforts that the Georgian writers, she and her friends, have made to tell the truth and the struggle to do so given the outmoded tools they have inherited. James Joyce, she writes, is like a man who breaks the window in order to breathe. "We must reflect," she continues, "that where so much strength is spent on finding a way of telling the truth, the truth itself is bound to reach us in rather an exhausted and chaotic condition." Several pages of the essay are devoted to the contract between writer and reader. She urges readers to be more demanding: "Your part is to insist that writers shall come down off their plinths and pedestals, and describe beautifully if possible, truthfully at any rate, our Mrs. Brown . . . But do not expect just at present a complete and satisfactory presentment of her."

When she gave this talk, Woolf had not yet embarked on *To the Lighthouse*, but her words offer a helpful insight into her view of the role of the reader. Readers need to demand beauty and truth, but they do not get to demand that novelists take care of them, or make things easy. In a letter to her brother-in-law, Clive Bell, Woolf perceptively remarked, "I feel I have so few of the gifts that make novels amusing." She is aware that, ideally, the reader needs to be entertained, but much more important is to convey the complexity of experience. The description of Mr. Ramsay's arrival at the lighthouse is a good example of her ambition and her accomplishment: "He rose and stood in the bow of the boat, very straight and tall, for all the world, James thought, as if he were saying: 'There is no God,' and Cam thought, as if he were leaping into space, and they both rose to follow him as he sprang, lightly like a young man, holding his parcel, on to the rock." To make this moment complete, Woolf needs to show the points of view of James, Cam, and an omniscient narrator. We inhabit her characters at the deepest level, following her from one consciousness to the next, even while we know almost none of the conventional facts about them. Woolf does not believe in exposition but she does believe, passionately, in consciousness, connection, and completeness.

This aesthetic agenda also makes clear why her best known novels, *Mrs Dalloway* and *To the Lighthouse*, cover such short periods of time; a single day in the former, and a handful of hours, plus ten years, in the latter. In "A Sketch of the Past" Woolf writes, "The present when backed by the past is a thousand times deeper than the present when it presses so close that you can feel nothing else." She does not have time for conventional plots that require the passage of days and weeks. The excitement and importance of the novel, for Woolf, lies in the depth to which it can allow us to enter into the consciousness of her characters, and to see the world through their eyes. How can sentences, one following another, hope to convey that everyone, at almost every moment, is experiencing simultaneously so many things?

Many of us, as writers, probably need more external story than Woolf offers in her major fiction. She has almost no interest in conventional plot and suspense but she is very interested in the larger seismic shifts of society. In "Mr. Bennett and Mrs. Brown" she claims, "All human relations have shifted—those between masters and servants, husbands and wives, parents and children. And when human relations change there is at the same time a change in religion, conduct, politics and literature." In her efforts to portray these changes, she shows us how to be ambitious for our work. Although we write in our own very different forms, we can share her goals of creating complex, contradictory characters, of portraying a new sensibility that reveals the new reality, and of writing sentences that might elicit the kind of admiration that Clive Bell offers to hers. "What is Virginia doing now," he writes, "at half past three o'clock. Moulding one of those delicately tangible sentences which remind me of nothing so much as a live bird in the hand, the heart beating through tumultuously."

In workshops and in private conversations my students seldom appeal to a larger aesthetic vision to justify their choices. Indeed the most common defense of fiction remains the oxymoron: this really happened. It's easy to imagine the first thirty pages of *To the Lighthouse* faring poorly in a workshop discussion, and not through any fault of the participants; the pages are difficult, sometimes confusing, and often demanding. But it's also easy to imagine Woolf defending the pages, pointing to what she thinks fiction should accomplish, showing how her sentences fulfill those demands. Here she is, in 1926, in the thick of *To the Lighthouse*, writing to Sackville-West:

> Style is a very simple matter; it is all rhythm.
> Once you get that, you can't use the wrong
> words . . . Now this is very profound, what

> rhythm is, and goes far deeper than words. A sight, an emotion, creates this wave in the mind, long before it makes words to fit it; and in writing (such is my present belief) one has to recapture this, and set this working (Which has nothing apparently to do with words) and then, as it breaks and tumbles in the mind, it makes words to fit it.

Given this amazing ambition, to make a wave in the mind—"the sea is to be heard all through it"—Woolf's style is surprisingly simple.

I find the argument that Woolf presents in "Mr. Bennett and Mrs. Brown" very persuasive, but it is interesting to note that a large part of the essay is a beautiful and very conventional character sketch of Mrs. Brown and her interactions with Mr. Smith. We see Mrs. Brown with her tidy threadbare clothes and clean little boots; we hear her speak; we speculate about her thoughts, her feelings, and her history:

> "Can you tell me if an oak-tree dies when the leaves have been eaten for two years in succession by caterpillars?"
>
> She spoke quite brightly, and rather precisely, in a cultivated, inquisitive voice.

> Mr. Smith was startled, but relieved to
> have a safe topic of conversation given him.
> He told her a great deal very quickly . . .
> While he talked a very odd thing happened.
> Mrs. Brown took out her little white hand-
> kerchief and began to dab her eyes. She was
> crying.

Paragraph after paragraph, the descriptions build and deepen and complicate in smoothly written prose. But Woolf herself claims that Mrs. Brown has slipped through her fingers; she has shirked the arduous task of getting her on the page. In *To the Lighthouse*, the narrator seldom presents her characters with such clarity. She refuses to sum them up but instead enters into them at the deepest, murkiest level. We are wading through the rag-and-bone shop of the mind and heart. We see them as they see themselves; we see them as others see them. Forget the impressionists and think of Picasso depicting a woman's face, fractured, from several angles.

The idea for *To the Lighthouse* may have been suggested to Woolf by the shades of her dead parents, but she was adamant that she did not want to write fiction that was solely biographical or autobiographical. The novel had to be about something more, something larger—an elegy not only for two individuals but also for Europe before the war. And, in the figure of Lily Briscoe, an artist and the main observer of the struggle between Mrs. Ramsay's intuitions and Mr. Ramsay's reasons, she was also able to question the whole notion of representation and of how experience is conveyed from one person to another. Woolf thought the novel was the best thing she ever wrote, and when it was done she noticed something remarkable. From the ages of thirteen to forty-four she had been obsessed with her mother, but after writing *To the Lighthouse*, her mother disappeared. "I no longer hear her voice," she wrote. "I do not see her." The novel turned out to be not only an elegy but also an exorcism.

If she were alive and writing now, Woolf would surely be pondering the many shifts in consciousness that have occurred since the Second World War. She would be writing and arguing about what it means to write in a time of such interconnectedness, when news flashes around the world in minutes, when many more people feel free to experiment with the shifting nature of sexual identity, when issues of race, class, religion, and citizenship are more complicated and vexed than ever before, when nature and climate can no longer be safely taken for granted. She would be teaching us how to resist the platitudes of thought and feeling that we sometimes succumb to, and to keep questioning the gap between lived experience and the page. Now more than ever, when so many writers are at work, it behooves us to figure out what we value in fiction, what we are writing toward, and against, and how our work can more accurately capture the chaos of experience in the golden net of consciousness. "Nothing was simply one thing."

NEITHER A BORROWER NOR A LENDER BE

Paying Homage

Neither a borrower nor a lender be;
For loan oft loses both itself and friend,
And borrowing dulls the edge of husbandry.

—Polonius, *Hamlet*

EZRA POUND'S "make it new" is one of the most famous commandments of twentieth-century art and, like much great advice, is more complicated than it at first seems. When I began to write, I interpreted him to be urging originality. A story was not worth writing if it didn't have a fresh and surprising plot; I had not yet discovered the possibilities of prose. If I had looked at Pound's own work, full of translations and reworkings, I would have realized that the "it" in "make it new" is not so much the "world" as "art" and that Pound is saying much the same thing as James Baldwin at the end of his story "Sonny's Blues." Baldwin's narrator is in a bar listening to his brother, Sonny, play the piano with a group of musicians, led by Creole:

> Creole began to tell us what the blues are
> all about. They were not about anything

very new. He and his boys up there were keeping it new, at the risk of ruin, destruction, madness, and death, in order to find new ways to make us listen. For, while the tale of how we suffer, and how we are delighted, and how we may triumph is never new, it always must be heard. There isn't any other tale to tell, it's the only light we've got in all this darkness.

Let me suggest, then, that one way to make both art and the world new, a way that would never have occurred to my younger self, is to consciously retell an old story.

Such retellings are referred to in various ways. Sometimes they are called "borrowing," or "reimagining," or "quoting." Sometimes they are called "homage," that elegant French term that points to the superiority of the original. The French critic Derrida, punning on ontology, uses the term "haunting." I love this image of the earlier work ghosting around in the background of the new. When done secretly, with intent to deceive, it is described in harsher terms as copying, or plagiarism, or theft. This kind of close borrowing has been with us for centuries, perhaps as long as people have been making art. Did the first cave painters copy each other's bison and horses?

✿

There are several large categories of homage. First, the one we immediately recognize, is the faithful, foregrounded, unmistakable homage. One of the best-known contemporary examples is Jane Smiley's novel *A Thousand Acres*, in which almost every scene of *King Lear* is transposed to a farm in 1970s Iowa. From the opening pages, when Larry Cook decides to divide his land among his three daughters, we are aware of the novel's ambition. As we read further, it becomes apparent that Smiley is not merely nodding toward her original, or using it as a starting point, but following the plot in almost every detail. For many readers a significant part of the suspense of *A Thousand Acres* comes from wondering how she will re-create, or navigate, Shakespeare's great moments—Gloucester's blinding, for instance, or the storm scene—in the Iowa countryside.

A much earlier version of the faithful homage can be seen in Sir Walter Raleigh's poem "The Nymph's Reply to the Shepherd." Writing in 1600, Raleigh is responding to Christopher Marlowe's poem of the previous year: "The Passionate Shepherd to His Love." Marlowe's shepherd offers his beloved the conventional pleasures:

And we will sit upon the Rocks,
Seeing the Shepherds feed their flocks,
By shallow Rivers to whose falls
Melodious birds sing Madrigals.

And I will make thee beds of Roses
And a thousand fragrant posies,
A cap of flowers, and a kirtle
Embroidered all with leaves of Myrtle;

The shepherd continues to propose his list of gifts and enchantments without irony, in fiercely end-stopped iambic pentameter, and ends on exactly the same note as he began:

The Shepherds' Swains shall dance and sing
For thy delight each May-morning:
If these delights thy mind may move,
Then live with me, and be my love.

Raleigh's nymph, however, is not fooled for a second. Her poem opens with a syllogism:

If all the world and love were young,
And truth in every Shepherd's tongue,
These pretty pleasures might me move,

To live with thee, and be thy love.

But, alas, this antecedent is manifestly false. The world is neither young nor truthful, and the nymph goes on to dismiss the shepherd's blandishments not calmly or humorously, but savagely—"Time drives the flocks from field to fold, / When Rivers rage and Rocks grow cold, / And *Philomel* becometh dumb"—until her last irrefutable quatrain:

> But could youth last, and love still breed,
> Had joys no date, nor age no need,
> Then these delights my mind might move
> To live with thee, and be thy love.

Just for a moment Raleigh allows us to glimpse that, even while he mocks and destroys Marlowe's idyll, he wishes the world were more like the shepherd's than the nymph's. His poem is overt in its argument and it demonstrates one of the truths of homage: namely that writing back, even when done as faithfully as in *A Thousand Acres*, nearly always involves a critique of the original, or at least casts it in a new light. It is not possible to explore how every art form borrows and quotes, but looking at visual art we find many examples of homage, from the faithful to the subversive. Among the more faithful, I would suggest, is Manet's *Olympia*, which pays homage to Titian's *Venus of Urbino*. More than three hundred years later, Manet makes us look at Titian's masterpiece in a new way.

Faithful borrowing, however, is not always immediately obvious. In *The Story of Edgar Sawtelle*, David Wroblewski also turns to Shakespeare but does so in a much more covert fashion than Smiley. The novel is set in a dog kennel in northern Wisconsin, and most readers only slowly become aware that the account of Edgar's family, and the famous Sawtelle dogs they breed, is a reenactment of *Hamlet*. Edgar's favorite dog, the amazing Almondine, plays the part of Ophelia, and suffers a similar fate. Other characters and events map onto the play with similarly tragic results. This kind of gradual revelation demands more space than a poem, or even a long story, can provide.

A second category of homage is the much less faithful, slantways retelling that still makes clear the borrowing and still, despite departures from the original, follows the same arc. We begin and end in roughly the same place but for many pages we are mostly oblivious to the original. In her novel *Foreign Bodies*, Cynthia Ozick pays lively tribute to Henry James's *The Ambassadors*. Her heroine—the clever, courageous Bea Nightingale—steps with aplomb into Lambert Strether's shoes as she

Venus of Urbino, Titian, 1538

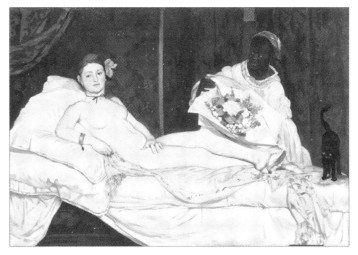

Olympia, Édouard Manet, 1865

takes to the streets of Paris in an attempt to rescue her nephew. Similarly, in "Gold Boy, Emerald Girl" Yiyun Li transposes William Trevor's "Three People" from Ireland to Beijing. In Trevor's story an elderly man, living alone with his surviving daughter, hopes that the young man who visits the house to do odd jobs will marry her. In Li's story a mother urges her son, a gay man in his forties, to marry one of her former students. The secrets in the two stories are very different but the arc and the somber tone are similar. Li, like Trevor, allows us to understand all three points of view. Patricia Park, in her novel *Re Jane*, also works a clever transposition. She sets her version of *Jane Eyre* mostly in a Korean American community in New York and lets the reader figure out for herself that the feminist literary critic, writing away at the top of the house, is a version of Mrs. Rochester.

We can see this kind of relationship at work in another pair of poems: Sir Philip Sidney's sonnet "With how sad steps" from *Astrophil and Stella* and Philip Larkin's "Sad Steps."

> With how sad steps, O moon, thou
>   climb'st the skies!
> How silently, and with how wan a face!
> What! May it be that even in heavenly
>   place

That busy archer his sharp arrows tries?
Sure, if that long-with-love-acquainted eyes
Can judge of love, thou feel'st a lover's case:
I read it in thy looks: thy languished grace
To me, that feels the like, thy state decries.
Then, even of fellowship, O Moon, tell me,
Is constant love deemed there but want of wit?
Are beauties there as proud as here they be?
Do they above love to be loved, and yet
Those lovers scorn whom that love doth
    possess?
Do they call 'virtue' there—ungratefulness?

Several centuries later Larkin signals with his title "Sad Steps" that he is writing back to Sidney, but then uses the vernacular of his opening line—"Groping back to bed after a piss"—to make us forget. The poem describes the speaker parting the curtains and being startled to discover "the moon's cleanliness." He goes on to make fun, in increasingly high diction, of the ways in which poets have addressed the moon: "Lozenge of love! Medallion of art!" But then he too, in the last stanza, succumbs to the moon's power: it is, he tells us "a reminder of the strength and pain / Of being young: that it can't come again, / But is for others undiminished somewhere."

Larkin, like Sidney, has reached a position of high melancholy on the subject of romantic love, although his stance is one of a noncombatant, looking back from middle age, whereas Sidney is still in the thick of battle. The "undiminished" of Larkin's last line gracefully echoes Sidney's "ungratefulness." Like Raleigh's poem to Marlowe, Larkin's poem is both homage and reply but it is also very much its own work of art, one that can be appreciated by readers with no inkling of its ancestor.

A third category of homage is the retelling from a different point of view. This is almost invariably subversive and has grown increasingly popular in the last half century. Tom Stoppard's 1966 play *Rosencrantz and Guildenstern Are Dead*, which puts the two minor messengers in *Hamlet* center stage, is one of the best-known examples. Stoppard makes riotous fun of the messengers, and of the canonical play, while also showing us their deaths, which *Hamlet* barely mentions. Jean Rhys's *Wide Sargasso Sea* was published the same year and has a darker purpose. The novel is mostly a prequel to *Jane Eyre* told partly from the point of view of the young Mrs. Rochester and partly from the point of view of Rochester himself. Writing in the first person, Rhys finds a sympathy for each character that is lacking in the original. Not long after *Jane Eyre* was published, Charlotte Brontë expressed regret for her depiction of Bertha Rochester; we should pity the mad, she claimed, not demonize them. Rhys follows this advice. She renames Bertha "Antoinette" and gives her a complicated history, making her an outcast twice over—in her family, and in the Caribbean society that labels her "a white cockroach." As for Rochester, he becomes the beleaguered younger son, coerced into marrying for money. The novel was embraced not only as literary homage but also as a piercing story of the corrupt power of colonial England. In visual art we see the same kind of relationship between the Spanish painter Velázquez's portrait of Pope Innocent X, painted around 1650, and the British painter Francis Bacon's series of screaming popes, painted in the 1950s. Bacon repeatedly questions, mocks, sabotages, and denounces the power and privilege of the original.

There are also more playful kinds of homage, which both acknowledge the original and depart radically from it. Julian Barnes's *Flaubert's Parrot* does not aspire to retell Flaubert's *A Simple Heart* but offers a witty exploration of that novella as well as of *Madame Bovary* and of Flaubert's life. In a somewhat similar fashion Michael Cunningham's *The Hours* both follows the plot of *Mrs Dalloway* and draws on the life of Virginia Woolf.

The last category of homage I want to mention comes from the eloquent literary and cultural critic

Portrait of Pope Innocent X, Diego Velázquez, 1650

Roberto Calasso. According to Calasso, James Joyce's *Ulysses* is not a retelling of *The Odyssey* so much as a reimagining of the myth of Odysseus, which has no single author and has been repeated over the centuries in various forms. Myths, legends, and fairy tales, he suggests, are owned in common and are available to everyone. Calasso also cites some singly authored works that have achieved this mythic status. Daniel Defoe's

Study after Velázquez's Portrait of Pope Innocent X,
Francis Bacon, 1953

Robinson Crusoe, for example, has been retold or subverted by Elizabeth Bishop, Derek Walcott, Michel
Tournier, and J. M. Coetzee, among others. These reimaginings simultaneously call the original into question and reflect its status in the culture.

Looking at these examples of homage, a couple
of criteria immediately become apparent. The earlier
work is usually well known, if not canonical, and the

borrowing is not a secret, guilty or otherwise. In his 2007 essay "The Ecstasy of Influence," the novelist Jonathan Lethem describes a story published in Germany in 1916. It follows a cultivated middle-aged man who, while traveling, rents a room and proceeds to fall in love with his landlord's daughter. Despite her age—she is not yet thirteen—the relationship is consummated. Then the girl dies, and the man is left alone forever. The title of this eponymous story is "Lolita." Lethem speculates as to whether Nabokov's borrowing was conscious. Certainly his use of the name suggests that he was not trying to hide his debts. Still this does not, for me, count as homage. Nabokov did not expect his poorly educated American readers to know a story published in Europe forty years earlier; he was not relying on that tension between his work and the original. And of course what is most essential in *Lolita*, the gorgeous, driving voice— "light of my life, fire of my loins"—is entirely his own.

Looking at any longer list of retellings also makes clear that Shakespeare is a special case of a single author whose work has become mythic. He himself famously borrowed many of his plots, and it seems only fair that his work is so widely the subject of homage that a whole industry has sprung up around these forays into intertextuality. This torrent of borrowings also means that, when appropriating Shakespeare, an author faces the additional burden of being compared not only with the original but also with the works of fellow borrowers.

Which brings me to my own large, vested interest in this topic. Ten years ago, if I had been asked to expound on homage I would have done so with enthusiasm but with no particular axe to grind. I had secretly borrowed (or do I mean "appropriated"?) an image from the Scottish writer Lewis Grassic Gibbon here, an emotional transaction from Henry James there, but I had never attempted full-scale homage, and, while enjoying the reimaginings of other authors, I had no plans to enter such complicated territory. But in 2008 I began to write a reimagining of a novel that has never been out of print since it was first published in 1847, and which, as I've mentioned, was already the source for Rhys's iconic homage: *Jane Eyre.*

Writing a novel is hard enough. Why write in the shadow of a masterpiece? I cannot entirely trace the route by which my answer to this question changed from "Good point. I won't" to "Because I must," but I can name some significant stages on my journey. In my novel *The House on Fortune Street* one of my characters is doing his PhD on Keats. Rereading Keats's poems and his passionate, lively letters was a delight, and I relished the challenge of trying to weave glimpses of the poet's work and too-short life into my narrative. Once I finished this section of the novel I began to ponder whether I could do something similar for my three other main characters and give each of them what I decided to call a "literary godparent," an author whose work and life addresses their deeper preoccupations.

This was my first venture into thinking as a writer—rather than as a reader, or a critic, or a teacher—about literary borrowing and what it could do for my fiction. I had two rules for my godparents. They would be well-known nineteenth-century British writers, and almost everything the reader needs to know about them, and the text being referenced, would be in the narrative. While I enjoyed working on this aspect of the novel, I did not finish *Fortune Street* thinking, now I want to attempt a full-scale homage of one of my favorite novels. I first read *Jane Eyre* the summer I was nine years old and living in the grounds of the boys' private school in Scotland where my father taught. I chose the novel from his bookshelves because it had a girl's name on the spine, and when I opened it—good news!—it turned out to be about a girl almost my age. As I kept reading, I found several more reasons to identify with Jane. The Scottish moors were surely not so different from the Yorkshire moors, and the school where my father taught—it was founded the same year that *Jane Eyre* was published—was a Gothic building with battlements and attics, an excellent stand-in for

Thornfield Hall. Closer to home, my severe stepmother bore a strong resemblance to Jane's aunt. Soon after I read the novel I gained an additional reason for empathizing with Jane when we moved to the south of Scotland and I too was sent to a dreadful girls' school.

Since that first passionate reading, I have reread the novel a number of times, for pleasure and to teach. Certain events in Jane's life are more real than events in my own. Soon after I published *Fortune Street*, I once again reread *Jane Eyre* in order to meet with a book club in Boston. The room that night was full of passionate readers, and here was the thing that struck me: although no one admitted to having a difficult stepmother, or growing up in the shadow of a Gothic boys' school, or attending a dreadful girls' school, everyone had entered into Jane's story. And everyone seemed to understand, however inchoately, that the reason Jane cannot marry Rochester the first time is not only because Mrs. Rochester's brother interrupts the ceremony. Jane cannot marry Rochester because she is not yet her own person.

Brontë herself may not have understood what she accomplished when a voice calls out in the church, "The marriage cannot go on: I declare the existence of an impediment." In writing this dramatic scene she satisfies the conventions of both the heroic novel, by which the heroine must face repeated trials, and the gothic novel, which demands dark coincidences. She also achieves a crucial deepening of her psychological themes.

As I drove home from the book club, I realized I had made a typical reader's mistake in thinking that the novel spoke to me because of the superficial similarities between my life and Jane's. That roomful of readers made clear that the real reason why the novel endures has much more to do with Brontë's skillful decisions. The year before she wrote *Jane Eyre*, she had written a novel titled *The Professor*, which drew on similar material: a romance between an older, more powerful man and a young woman, told in the first person from the point of view of the man. The novel was intended, along with Emily's *Wuthering Heights* and Anne's *Agnes Grey*, to be part of a triple-decker, a popular form of Victorian publishing. But while her sisters' novels were promptly accepted, *The Professor* was roundly rejected. Brontë began *Jane Eyre* in response to the nicest of the rejections, and first and foremost among her good decisions was to make her narrator a young woman not so different from herself, capable of remarkable passion and poetry. She wrote the opening pages while nursing her father through cataract surgery, an experience that may have led to her decision to blind Rochester later in the novel.

Several other critical choices contribute to the novel's enduring appeal. It is structured as a journey with five distinct settings, each with its own atmosphere and psychological arc. And Brontë makes Jane—small, plain Jane—the embodiment of two of our great archetypes: the pilgrim and the orphan. In his essay "Family Romances" Freud argues that children take refuge in the belief that they are orphans because on the one hand they feel slighted and on the other they begin to notice that their parents are less than perfect. These difficult people, the child thinks, are not my parents; my real parents are wonderful, talented aristocrats. Whatever the truth of Freud's theory—I never doubted that my difficult parents were mine—readers love orphans. Victorian literature is awash with them, and more recently *Harry Potter* and *The Goldfinch* prove that they still cast a powerful spell. The orphan's story, without parents to limit the imagination or provide a safety net, is all our stories writ large.

❄

Shortly after that evening at the book club, I hid my copy of *Jane Eyre* and sat down to ask again Brontë's great question: How is a girl with no particular talents, no means, and no family (that she knows of) to make her

Le Déjeuner sur l'herbe, Édouard Manet, 1863

Le Déjeuner sur l'herbe, Paul Cézanne, 1876

way in the world? Gemma Hardy, I decided, would be an orphan growing up in 1960s Scotland. I knew, almost from the first page, that I was not going to follow Smiley in faithfully and obviously updating the story, or even Wroblewski in doing so faithfully and subtly. Indeed so much have social and sexual mores changed, along with our attitudes to mental illness, that I am not sure such an enterprise is possible. I did briefly consider reversing Rochester's and Jane's roles, making them a young man and an older, more powerful woman, but (sadly) I worried about issues of plausibility. My hope was to be both faithful and faithless, somewhere between, say, Ozick and Smiley. I wanted Gemma to have her own story, even while she, in many respects, follows Jane's. To readers who know Brontë's work, I signaled my intentions by modeling my opening chapter on what I remembered of the beginning of *Jane Eyre*—the fight between Jane and her cousin and her banishment to the haunted red room. But in my second chapter, I departed radically from Brontë and gave Gemma an Icelandic childhood. If I had to choose a pair of paintings to illustrate my homage and its relationship to the original, it would perhaps be Manet's iconic *Le Déjeuner sur l'herbe* and one of Cézanne's several paintings by the same name.

Writing, for me, is always a roller coaster, and it was never more so than when working on *Gemma*

Hardy. On good days I felt that I was standing on the shoulders of a giant, but on bad days all I could see was the giant looming over me. A major challenge of homage, I discovered, is how to avoid irritating readers who know the original while at the same time including those who don't. My solution—still evolving—is a variation on reader response theory. Baldly summarized, reader response theory claims that readers complete the text in various ways and that that's all right. (The classical view argues that there is a single text and a single, correct interpretation.)

Putting theory aside, I would say that the question of how to include readers who know the original and those who don't is not so different from the question of how to include readers who know Poughkeepsie and those who don't, those who are parents and those who aren't, those who love horses and those who can't tell a hoof from a fetlock. Since the Second World War readers have been growing increasingly diverse; no writer now, in Europe or the States, can count on having a single unified audience. In a workshop I taught in Miami a few years ago I had twenty students from eleven different countries. We debated the meaning of such words as "home," "family," "love," "goodness."

In an effort to include as many readers as possible, let me summarize the plot of *Jane Eyre*: A ten-year-old girl, an orphan, is sent by her cruel aunt to a dreadful girls' school where she is hungry and cold and her best friend dies. Jane survives, and, at the age of eighteen, finds a job as a governess at Thornfield Hall. There she falls in love with her employer, the much older Mr. Rochester, and he with her. But on their wedding day Jane learns that there is already a Mrs. Rochester, a madwoman who is kept prisoner in the attic. She flees Thornfield Hall and after wandering for several days collapses, starving and penniless, on the doorstep of some kind people. She recovers, becomes the village schoolteacher, and narrowly escapes marriage with a man who does not love her. The novel ends in sweeping romantic fashion. Jane gains a family (the kind people turn out to be her cousins), money (a long-lost uncle dies), and the husband of her heart's desire: Rochester, now blind.

In its own small way, not remotely comparable to neurosurgery or NASCAR racing, making art is a risky business. In retelling a classic one faces not only the usual risks but also the particular challenge of how to negotiate the climactic scenes of the original: How can one hope to do them better? Or even half as well? Yet it seems impossible to write a reimagining without attempting a reprise of at least some of the key scenes. Others, however, are best subverted or ignored. Fairly early in my novel I recognized that re-creating Mrs.

Rochester in 1960s Scotland was, for me, an impossible task. There would be no attics in *Gemma Hardy*.

Some elements of the original, however, were too central to ignore. What would be the point of writing even a heavily camouflaged, or indirect, reimagining of *Jane Eyre* without a Rochester-like figure? If I wasn't going to depict a version of that central relationship, then I might as well exorcise Brontë's ghost and chart my own course. Every artist who attempts an homage has to find her or his own way to answer a version of these questions.

It was only when I was well into writing the novel that another truth also became apparent. Homage brings one up against not only the strengths of the original but also the shortcomings. Most readers remember the same dramatic episodes in *Jane Eyre*: the terrible school, the first meeting, the mad wife, the interrupted marriage, and the final reconciliation. All except the last take place in the first two parts of the novel. The third part, which shows Jane wandering on the moors, being rescued, fending off her suitor and his tedious religiosity, has its longueurs. What is the re-imaginer to do? I won't describe my attempts to answer this question, only point out that both the best and the worst parts of the original are problematic. Almost inevitably one is going to fall short of the former and one follows the latter too closely at one's peril.

Most writers also have to find a way to respond to the voice of their chosen text. Oddly, but perhaps understandably, writers who pay homage to Shakespeare seem to largely ignore this issue. But in *The Hours* Cunningham is clearly aware of Woolf's cadences. And in "Gold Boy, Emerald Girl" Li pays homage to Trevor not just in her plot but in her prose. In *Gemma Hardy* I tried to find a voice that is simultaneously *of* its time and place, and yet hovers slightly *above* that time and place. Then there was the additional challenge of the soaring language Jane uses in her great speeches to Rochester. Here is her response when he pretends that he's going to marry another woman and asks Jane to remain in his household:

> "I tell you I must go!" I retorted, roused to something like passion. "Do you think I can stay to become nothing to you? Do you think I am an automaton?—a machine without feelings? And can bear to have my morsel of bread snatched from my lips, and my drop of living water snatched from my cup? Do you think, because I am poor, obscure, plain, and little, I am soulless and heartless?—You think wrong!—I have as much soul as

you,—and full as much heart! And if
God had gifted me with some beauty, and
much wealth, I should have made it as
hard for you to leave me, as it is now for
me to leave you.

To describe Jane's outburst as "something like
passion" is a woeful understatement. Her poetry conquers both Mr. Rochester and the reader. No wonder
we don't stop to question the plausibility of a wealthy,
powerful, upper-class man falling in love with a poor,
plain, middle-class woman. And no wonder that to
write my reimagining I had to hide the original. Once
I had begun *Gemma Hardy*, I did not open my copy of
Jane Eyre for three years.

So once again I have to ask: Why embark on such a
hazardous enterprise? I put this question to the painter
Gerry Bergstein, whose painting adorns the cover of
this book and whose beautiful, witty work often draws
heavily on art history. He came up with eight answers:

1. To provide a contemporary update of
    older themes that often contradicts
    the original
2. Sheer love
3. To make a cultural critique

4. To demonstrate political, or other forms, of social evolution
5. To distill the earlier work
6. To develop the traditions of a beloved forebear
7. Any combination of the above
8. As a joke

When I questioned this last point, Bergstein showed me René Magritte's painting titled *Perspective: Madame Récamier by David*, in which the woman Jacques-Louis David portrayed in 1800 has been replaced by a coffin. Only the fall of white drapery suggests her presence.

I do think that #1, #2, #4, and #6 each played some part in my motivation. The idea of reexamining the possibilities for women's lives more than a century after Brontë wrote was one of several reasons why I set the novel in the 1960s, shortly before that great wave of feminism broke over both Europe and the States. At that time in Scotland there were four professions open to middle-class women—nurse, teacher, secretary, wife—two more than were open to Brontë and her sisters before they added "writer." And when a woman became a wife, the best of the professions, she almost invariably gave up her job outside the home. In writing *Gemma Hardy* I wanted to question those narrow expectations, and I wanted the reader to know that Gemma was growing up into a time of many more possibilities for women.

Most of Bergstein's reasons suggest that the artist writing back does so out of the loftiest of motives, but perhaps, for some borrowers, there is a less lofty side. One of the challenges I regularly face as a novelist is hearing a great story that, even as I reach for my notebook, I realize I can tell only at the risk of losing family, friends, or employment. *Jane Eyre* is a fantastic story: my adopted father, reading it for the first time, missed a landing strip during World War II because Rochester was about to propose. Of course the writer in me longed to steal it. Happily, I discovered that in homage outright theft is impossible. My debt to Brontë is unmistakable.

One other ambition accompanied me throughout my writing of the novel. I wanted Gemma to be not just a character but a heroine. Although small in stature and young in years, I wanted her to be larger than life. To that end I made her face dragons and demons and disasters. And, like Jane, she is truthful and opinionated. A heroine cannot simply sit at home, drinking cups of tea.

Finally, and I've thought about this long and hard, there is the question of suspense in literary homage. A few years ago in London I took an elderly friend to *Oedipus Rex*. Philip had accepted my invitation eagerly and as the lights went down he leaned forward.

Portrait of Madame Récamier, Jacques-Louis David

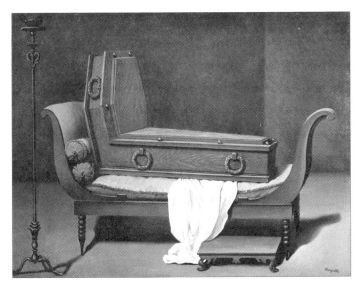

Perspective: Madame Récamier by David, René Magritte, 1949

Gradually, as he whispered—"But that's his mother!" "Don't do it!"—I realized he did not know the plot. He was on the edge of his seat about *what* was going to happen; I was on the edge of mine about *how* it was going to happen, and *why*. In the reimagined work the suspense for one group of readers comes partly from their very familiarity with the plot and the characters; for another it resides purely in the work itself, which is why the reimagining needs to be its own compelling story. The good news is that we value both kinds of suspense. Indeed some people would argue that the pleasure of revisiting is superior to that of the first encounter. When giving readings of her story "A Good Man Is Hard to Find," Flannery O'Connor always began by describing the plot in order to allow her listeners to pay attention to what really matters.

And that—what really matters—is surely the key to successful homage. As I hope I've made clear, I think Polonius is wrong, at least when it comes to art. We are not diminished or dulled by borrowing and lending. In the best homages the contemporary artist is able to plumb some aspect of her or his own deepest interests, to reach what really matters, while simultaneously agreeing with or repudiating, delighting in or detonating, the original work. I have come a long way from that house beside the Scottish moors where I first read *Jane Eyre* to the desk in

Cambridge, Massachusetts, where I now write. On my journey I have paid homage to several writers—they had no say in the way I borrowed their landscapes and their insights, their nightingales and their bad behavior. I hope in doing so to have brought attention to their work and, at the same time, I hope to have made something new.

GUSTAVE AND EMMA

Finding the First Novel

Artists: All hoaxers.

—FLAUBERT,
Dictionnaire des idées reçues

*For me a book has always only been a way of living
in some particular milieu. That is what explains
my hesitations, my anguish and my slowness.*

—FLAUBERT,
letter to Mlle. Leroyer de Chantepie,
December 26, 1858

I

EMMA BOVARY WOULD surely never have behaved as she did if she had read the novel that bears her name, but Charles Bovary, such is his feeling for her, might have. Or so it seems to me upon rereading the novel they share. Much has shifted in my own life during the decades since I first met them, and much has shifted in the novel. The rooms are the same but the views from the windows have vastly altered. Windows are important to Emma. Over and over she is depicted looking out, longing. Sometimes she sees a man she loves—Charles, Léon, Rodolphe, Léon again—but mostly what meets her gaze is the boredom of her father's farm or the dreary village of Tostes or the, initially, more promising town of Yonville. One of the great scenes in the novel, the courtship between Rodolphe and Emma, is set at a window in the town hall where they sit looking down on the agricultural fair. I, too, as I first read these pages, found myself looking out of windows, longing.

I had only just begun to write. Reading was all about pleasure, about having a wider world. I still—how strange this now seems—had no concept of learning from the novels I loved. I gave myself over to Emma's ardors and despairs, and entirely failed to notice how expertly Flaubert structures the novel, how deftly he moves the reader from one point of view to the next, how conscious he is of imagery and patterns, and how clearly he foreshadows the main events. The first time Charles visits Emma's father's farm, his horse, which plods along obligingly for the rest of the novel, shies in melodramatic fashion.

Not only did I not understand how the novel worked its magic, I also knew little about its author or why we might consider him our first modern novelist. I knew he was French, that the novel had been published in the 1850s, that Henry James had called Flaubert a "novelist's novelist." I was aware of some of his sweeping claims: "A writer should be in his work as God is in the physical universe—everywhere present and nowhere visible." "The only truth in the world is a well-made sentence." "Art requires a priestly devotion." (And in his own case, I would add, family money.) But I knew almost nothing about his life and how he had come to write such a magnificent "first" novel.

Nor did I know the degree to which the novel was the fruit of his devoted friendship with Louis Bouilhet, a poet and playwright. Novelists did not, at that time, have agents or editors to advise them. Most worked in solitude, and novels were either rejected or published. Flaubert was a deeply fortunate exception. Bouilhet urged him toward the subject matter of *Madame Bovary*, and visited almost every weekend to pore over the week's pages, usually no more than four or five, and suggest cuts, additions, and revisions. He encouraged Flaubert to give the novel the beauty and density one would normally find in a poem.

Neither my inability to read more deeply nor my ignorance of Flaubert's life and methods diminished my enthusiasm for the novel, but they did limit what I learned from that first encounter. Reading the novel again, in Lydia Davis's penetrating translation, knowing what I do now about both writing and Flaubert, I felt perhaps a little of what his most famous protégé, Guy de Maupassant, must have felt: here was a writer whose every page has something to teach me. When I reached the end, I was also struck by how much there is to learn from the way in which Flaubert drew on his own experiences in writing *Madame Bovary*.

The connection between craft and autobiography is one that almost invariably interests readers and yet remains, perhaps rightly, confusing for authors. While we recognize the superficial sources of our material, we are often among the last to apprehend the deeper psychic impulses that draw us to it. In the case of *Madame Bovary*, the plot came from a well-known local scandal. Delphine Delamare, the second wife of a health officer, had committed adultery, squandered her husband's money, and then poisoned herself. Flaubert already knew about the Delamares when Bouilhet suggested them as the subject of his next novel, but whether either man understood the degree to which Flaubert's history and nature would make him the ideal person to tell their story is a mystery.

First, there was his lifelong acquaintance with medical matters. Both his father and his older brother, Achilles, were doctors, and Flaubert grew up around the hospital in Rouen. Charles Bovary's profession and two of the main events in the novel—the disastrous operation on the stable boy and Emma's taking arsenic—owe much to this early familiarity with medicine. Perhaps the operation also owes something to the final illness of Flaubert' father. In November 1845 he complained of a pain in his thigh. It turned out to be an abscess. When other treatments failed, Achilles operated. The result was infection, gangrene, agony, and, in January 1846, death.

Flaubert's relationship with adultery was also long-standing. At the age of fifteen, while on holiday with his family at Trouville, he met an older, married woman—Elisa Schlesinger—on the beach. Their unconsummated relationship became one of the lodestars of his life. The following year he wrote "Passion and Virtue: A Philosophical Tale," about a married woman, Mazza, who daydreams about Ernest, a man she has seen at the Comédie Française. Ernest is utterly unworthy of her daydreams—"But he was an expert seducer; he knew by heart the devices, the tricks." Mazza gives herself to him body and soul, only to have him flee to Mexico. When her repulsive husband conveniently dies, she writes to Ernest. He writes back that he is already married, and she takes poison. Fifteen years later Rodolphe, Emma's first lover, talks and thinks like Ernest, while Emma shares Mazza's romantic daydreams.

More immediately, *Madame Bovary* was influenced by Flaubert's relationship with the poet Louise Colet, whom he met in 1846. She lived with her daughter in Paris, and even at the height of their relationship, the two seldom met. With some justice, Colet claimed that Flaubert would rather write to her than make love to her. We are the happy beneficiaries of his preference. Their ardent correspondence contains much of what we know about his working methods. And the character of Emma—as Flaubert, Bouilhet, and Colet each acknowledged—owes much to his mistress. Several critics, beginning with the poet Charles Baudelaire and including the philosopher Jean-Paul Sartre, have described Emma as a feminized man; she is too vigorous, too passionate, too active, they claim, to be a woman. But Flaubert knew better. She is modeled on Colet, who gave gifts, initiated meetings, made demands, and once even showed up at his home without invitation.

While Schlesinger's and Colet's roles in *Madame Bovary* are obvious, that of Flaubert's other lodestar, Alfred Le Poittevin, is less so. The two were family friends who became close when Le Poittevin was studying for his entrance exam to law school. Flaubert fell utterly under the older boy's spell. "We are ordained by Providence," he wrote, "to think and feel in harmony." Le Poittevin was a romantic of the highest order. The world is illusion; the past is infinitely superior to the present; man is a helpless toy in the hands of God; the life of the bourgeois, of *idées reçues*, is meaningless. He studied law to please his father, got married—"You are doing something abnormal," Flaubert wrote—to please his family. But Le Poittevin believed that to struggle against fate was useless. On April 3, 1848, with Flaubert at his bedside, he stopped struggling altogether. Flaubert never forgot his friend and never entirely relinquished his romantic ideals.

Flaubert's own health was a significant factor in his life and work. Like Le Poittevin, he was destined to become a lawyer. Then, during his first year of study, he had a seizure, lost consciousness, and fell out of a carriage. His parents brought him home, and any idea of his practicing law was abandoned. They purchased a house in the village of Croisset where Flaubert lived and wrote for most of his life. The seizures—they were similar to epilepsy but without the convulsions—gradually grew less frequent, but during them he experienced moments of intense awareness. He wrote: "I have an extraordinary faculty of perception"; and "Sometimes by dint of gazing at a pebble, an animal, a picture, I felt myself enter into them." As readers, we glimpse this gift in such passages as the one describing an early meeting between Charles and Emma:

> Once, during a thaw, the bark of the trees was oozing in the yard, the snow on the tops of the buildings was melting. She was on the doorsill; she went to get her parasol, she opened it. The parasol, of dovegrey iridescent silk, with the sun shining through it, cast moving glimmers of light

over the white skin of her face. She was
smiling beneath it in the mild warmth;
and they could hear the drops of water,
one by one, falling over the taut moiré.

Prior to embarking on his law studies, Flaubert had
written not only "Passion and Virtue" but also several
other short narratives. Now that he was free, he devoted
himself to writing and travel. He wrote a book about
exploring Brittany with his friend Maxime Du Camp
and early versions of two novels he would later revise
and publish: *A Sentimental Education* and *The Temptation of St. Anthony*. *The Temptation* was written at a furious pace in the eighteen months following Le Poittevin's
death, and is heavily influenced by their shared romantic ideals. In September 1849, over the course of four
days, Flaubert read the entire manuscript, all 541 pages,
aloud to Bouilhet and Du Camp. He finished at close
to midnight on the fourth day. According to Du Camp:

> Flaubert pounded his fist on the table.
> 'Now,' he cried. 'Tell me frankly what you
> think!' Bouilhet was naturally timid, but
> no one could express himself more fear-
> lessly when he had once made up his mind
> to speak. It was he who replied. 'We think

you should throw it into the fire, and never speak of it again.'

Flaubert jumped from his chair with a
cry of horror.

The two friends argued with Flaubert for hours,
pointing out the many problems in the novel. Finally
he took their words to heart; *The Temptation* joined its
predecessor in the drawer. Only in the sense of publication was *Madame Bovary* his first novel.

I mention these autobiographical facts as an element of Flaubert's craft, an element we can learn from.
We always bring some part of ourselves to even our
most purely imagined work. Awareness of this may not
be helpful as we generate material, but as we begin to
shape it, recognizing when and how our autobiographical sources are causing us to dwell at inappropriate
length on certain moments or, alternatively, to give
them short shrift is crucial. We can see how Flaubert's
intimacy with medical matters led him to write expan-
sively about the stable boy's operation and Emma's slow
death. In his original plan for the novel there is no mention of the former. About Emma he writes, "Death agony—precise medical details—'On such and such a day
at three o'clock in the morning her vomiting returned,'
etc." And of course Homais, Charles and Emma's

meddlesome neighbor in Yonville, became one of his favorite characters—"my pharmacist," he called him in letters. He cut many pages of his conversation and, for the modern reader's taste, might have cut still more.

Although Flaubert argued and protested when Bouilhet first suggested that Delphine Delamare should be the basis of his next novel—the story was too bourgeois, too vulgar—he was eventually persuaded. Five years after he set to work, he declared *Madame Bovary* finished, and in the autumn of 1856, Du Camp offered to serialize it in the magazine he edited: *La Revue de Paris.* The process of publication proved torturous and at many points Flaubert was ready to withdraw the novel. But finally the date for the first installment was set. He wrote to Bouilhet, "I lose my virginity as unpublished writer a week from Thursday, October first. May *fortuna virilis* be favourable to me!" *Fortuna* was not, at least according to Flaubert. Numerous typographical errors had escaped the printers, but worse, much worse, was the sight of his prose in print. "It seems utterly flat to me," he wrote again to Bouilhet. "Everything in it seems bad. This is literally true. It is a bitter disappointment, and the success of the book will have to be deafening indeed to cover the voice of my conscience, which keeps shouting: 'Failure! Failure!'"

But Bouilhet, who had applied himself so assiduously to the novel, was vindicated. From its opening pages *Madame Bovary* was a success: a novel that moved and excited readers. It also rapidly became a scandal. In an attempt to avoid being taken to court, the magazine, without telling Flaubert, cut the famous coach ride, when Léon and Emma hurtle round the streets of Rouen, and in the last installment, despite his vehement objections, cut numerous other scenes. But the censorship, as he predicted, made no difference. "You have seized upon the details," he wrote to the managing editor of the magazine, "whereas it is the book as a whole that is to blame. The brutal element is everywhere, not merely on the surface." In January 1857 Flaubert found himself in court, charged with offending public morality and religion.

All this was so upsetting that he was ready to put the novel away with the others in the drawer until Bouilhet reminded him that publication would allow him to restore the censored passages. *Madame Bovary*, dedicated to the lawyer who successfully defended it and to the faithful Bouilhet, was published in its entirety in April 1857 to excellent sales and many reviews. Was Flaubert at last pleased? Not entirely. "All this uproar around my first book," he wrote, "seems so irrelevant to Art that it sickens me, it dazes me. How I miss the fish-like silence in which I had persisted until now." Later he would also come to resent the success of his "first" novel, which overshadowed, both then and now, everything else he wrote.

II

Flaubert drew skillfully on his own life, listened to Bouilhet, and worked hard, but none of these—as he knew—guaranteed success. In the aftermath of his failures, he became our first modern writer, working in a self-conscious way and acutely aware of what his prose could do for his vulgar plot. "Continuity constitutes style," he wrote, "as constancy makes for virtue." The famous voice did not come to him easily. "My novel is having a frightful time getting started," he wrote to Colet. "I have abscesses of style, I itch with sentences that never appear . . . I am so disconsolate about the whole thing that I greatly enjoy it . . . The tone in which I am steeping myself is so new to me that I keep opening my eyes in astonishment." This time he heeded Du Camp and Bouilhet's advice that a perfect paragraph followed by a perfect paragraph followed by a perfect paragraph does not necessarily make three perfect paragraphs. A novel has to flow; the joints must not show. He also struggled with the banality of his characters' dialogue. Writing about the first meeting between Emma and

Léon, he remarked that he thought it was the first time a novel had made fun of its leading man and lady. "Irony," he added, "takes nothing away from pathos."

And he understood at last, painfully, the need for relevance. Every element in the novel must serve a purpose, ideally more than one. At Bouilhet's urging, after several attempts, he wrote a plan. It focuses mostly on the ups and downs of Emma's love life. The ball of part one and the agricultural fair of part two are mentioned, but only a clause in the last paragraph—"discovery of appalling debts"—hints at the role money will play in her downfall. This search for externals, the need to find an outer life, a wardrobe, if you will, for our characters, is a common task. Whatever the starting point of a novel—a public or private story, a resonant image, a memory—as we write, we keep searching for ways to dramatize the inner lives of our characters. Long before T. S. Eliot urged the need for an objective correlative—an object or an action to stand in for the emotions—Flaubert knew that he could not rely on the lyricism and imagery that had fatally marred *The Temptation.* Emma's inner life must be revealed by the details of her world, by her actions, and by the many minor characters.

Between my first and subsequent readings of *Madame Bovary*, I had remembered almost everything about Emma and her lovers, but I was shocked, as I began to read again, to find that the novel opens with Charles. Flaubert labored long and hard over the beginning. Everything about these pages was considered and reconsidered, including the detailed description of the extraordinary hat Charles is wearing when he arrives at school. "It was one of those headgears of a composite type, in which one may recognize elements of the busby, the lancer's shapska, the bowler, the otter-skin cap, and the cotton housecap, one of those sorry things, indeed, whose mute ugliness has depths of expression like the face of an imbecile." What kind of man is married to a woman who behaves like Emma? Flaubert answers this question promptly, showing Charles, an inept only child, oppressed first at home, then at school, then by his medical studies. After initially failing his exams, he becomes a medical officer (not—Flaubert was sensitive to such nuances—a doctor). His parents marry him to a much older widow, and he begins to practice in the village of Tostes. One day he is summoned to set a farmer's broken leg and meets the farmer's daughter, Emma. Typically unaware of his own longing, he begins to visit the farm. At a breakneck speed, reminiscent of "Passion and Virtue," Flaubert describes how Charles's wife forbids his visits; how it emerges that she has lied about her fortune; and how she conveniently dies.

At first we see Emma, as Charles does, in fragments: a shoulder here, a flounce there. Not until she is married and arrives at the house in Tostes do we see her whole and enter her consciousness. On the desk by the window she notices a bunch of orange flowers: "It was a bridal bouquet, the other woman's bouquet!" What will become of her own bouquet, Emma wonders dreamily, should she die. From then on she is at the center of the novel, but we still—and again this was a crucial decision on Flaubert's part—get Charles's point of view, as well as that of other characters and of our omniscient narrator. Here, for example, is Emma on her first evening in Yonville:

> The fire shone on her fully, penetrating with a raw light the weave of her dress, the regular pores of her white skin, and even her eyelids, which she closed from time to time. A bright red glow passed over her each time a gust of wind came through the half-open door.
>
> From the other side of the fireplace, a young man with fair hair was watching her in silence.
>
> Because he was very bored in Yonville, where he worked as a clerk for the lawyer Guillaumin, Monsieur Léon Dupuis . . .

We watch Emma, we see who is watching her, then we begin to learn about the watcher.

In Flaubert's original plan for *Madame Bovary* Léon plays a central role, but many other elements of the finished novel are missing. Only in the writing does he seem to have discovered the three-part structure. Each part marks a change in the setting. Within that structure he makes another brilliant choice: in each part he includes a large public event or space. In part one there is the ball, the life Emma longs for; in part two, the agricultural fair, the life from which she longs to escape; in part three, the cathedral that, in her convent girlhood, had seemed to promise a refuge. Each advances the plot and helps to develop what Flaubert calls "the different adventures of Emma's soul."

Long before the ball it is apparent that Emma and Charles are ill suited. Charles, who has stoically endured his first marriage, is transformed by "the continuous flow of . . . happiness" he finds in his second, but Emma is still searching for the marvelous passion she read about in novels at school: "a great rosyfeathered bird hovering in the splendor of a poetical sky." Instead of a rosy bird, however "boredom, that silent spider" takes up residence. The ball, at which Emma enjoys great success, briefly rescues her. At one point Flaubert considered having her infidelities begin that evening. His decision not to only renders more painful her glimpse of the life to which she feels she was born. In the aftermath of that glittering evening she feigns illness, and persuades Charles to leave Tostes, where his practice is doing well, and move to Yonville. In Yonville Léon is waiting with his own boredom.

Earlier novelists made use of juxtaposition—Jane Austen is particularly skillful at it—but Flaubert, committed to his belief that the author should not overtly comment on the action, relies frequently on this method of guiding the reader. Here are a few lines from the scene where Emma and Rodolphe are seated at the window, looking down at the agricultural fair while the prizes are being awarded:

> "A few days ago, for example, when I came to your house . . ." [Rodolphe says.]
>
> "To Monsieur Bizet, of Quincampoix—"
>
> "Did I know that I would be coming here with you?"
>
> "Seventy francs!"
>
> "A hundred times I've tried to leave you, and yet I've followed you, I've stayed with you."
>
> "For manures—"

> "As I would stay with you tonight, to-morrow, every day, my whole life!"
>
> "To Monsieur Caron, of Argueil, a gold medal!"

Ten pages later, when Rodolphe seduces Emma, Flaubert describes her as seeing the woods around them filled with beauty: "Something sweet seemed to be coming from the trees; she could feel . . . her blood flowing through her flesh like a river of milk." The lyrical paragraph ends with the sentence "Rodolphe, cigar between his teeth, mended with his penknife one of the bridles which was broken."

In *The Art of Fiction* John Gardner includes a list of exercises. One is to describe a barn from the point of view of a man who has just lost his son in the war without mentioning either the son or the war. Flaubert is a master of this technique, using specific details to create, simultaneously, the outer and the inner life. Here is Emma at the height of her despair in Tostes:

> But it was above all at mealtimes that she could not bear it any longer, in that little room on the ground floor, with the stove that smoked, the door that creaked, the

> walls that seeped, the damp flag stones; all
> the bitterness of life seemed to be served up
> on her plate, and, with the steam from the
> boiled beef, there rose from the depths of
> her soul other gusts of revulsion. Charles
> took a long time eating; she would nibble
> a few walnuts, or, leaning on her elbow,
> pass the time drawing lines on the oilcloth
> with the tip of her knife.

As he did earlier, when describing Emma on the doorsill with Charles, Flaubert uses intense perceptions to convey intense emotion. Then the bark was oozing, the snow was melting, the world full of possibility. Now the stove smokes, the door creaks, the walls seep. He catalogues the dreariness of that little room, and its effect on Emma, yet he does so without suggesting that she is consciously making the catalogue.

Although Flaubert knew Emma's fate before he embarked on the novel, it is crucial to the success of *Madame Bovary* that she does not enter easily into adultery. Over and over she seeks to escape the choices she finally makes. One of the most obvious escape routes—motherhood—is blocked almost immediately. Emma arrives in Yonville pregnant and longing for a son. "A man, at least, is free; he can explore every passion, every

land, overcome obstacles, taste the most distant pleasures. But a woman is continually thwarted . . . there
is always some desire luring her on, some convention
holding her back." Of course, she means a rich man,
like Rodolphe; poor Charles has never been free. When
he breaks the news to her that they have a daughter,
Emma faints. She christens the baby Berthe, a name she
overheard at the ball, but she never grows fond of her.
For the remainder of the novel, her daughter plays little
part in her thoughts or actions.

Being a mother offers no safety. Nor does the
church on the two occasions when Emma explicit-
ly asks for help. The first time is when she discovers
that Léon loves her. She is thrilled; she trembles at the
sound of his footsteps; she takes pride in being virtuous; she is tormented by desire and melancholy. In the
hope that he will help her to resist temptation, she goes
to talk to the curé:

> "How are you faring?" [the curé] added.
>
> "Not well," answered Emma; "I'm in
> pain."
>
> "Why, so am I," replied the clergy-
> man. "These first warm days weaken one
> terribly, don't they? Well, there's nothing
> to be done. We're born to suffer, as St.

Paul says. But, now, what does Monsieur Bovary think about this?"

"Oh, him," she said with a gesture of disdain.

"What!" replied the simple man, quite surprised; "hasn't he prescribed something for you?"

"Ah!" said Emma; "it isn't earthly remedies I need."

And so on for two more pages until, at last, she gives up:

"But you were asking me something, weren't you?" [the curé says.] "What was it? I can't remember."

"I? Oh, nothing . . . nothing . . . ," Emma repeated.

Even with no help from Berthe or the curé, she does manage to prevent Léon from making an explicit declaration. Not realizing that she shares his feelings, he wearies of her evasiveness and moves to Paris.

Her next suitor, Rodolphe, is older, wealthier, coarser, and much more sophisticated. He has no qualms about using on Emma the tricks and locutions that have worked so well with previous mistresses. Despite her delight in his overtures, she still tries to resist. She refuses to go riding with him until Charles urges her to accept the invitation for the good of her health. And there in the woods she joins the "lyrical host of adulterous women."

But soon, again, she is looking for escape. As it becomes increasingly clear that Rodolphe's passion does not match hers, she ponders a surprising possibility: "She even asked herself why she despised Charles, and whether it would not be better if she could love him." Enter Homais, the pharmacist, with his suggestion that Charles operate on the stable boy's clubfoot. Charles is nervous about the prospect—his main accomplishment is not to kill his patients—but Emma is optimistic: the operation will make him famous. "What a satisfaction it would be for her to have started him on a path that would increase both his reputation and his fortune? All she wanted, now, was to be able to lean on something more solid than love." She does not love Charles, but if he became successful and could give her the life she wants, then maybe the rosyfeathered bird wouldn't matter so much. And Flaubert, who has written so eloquently about her longing for romance, respects this new feeling. Who wouldn't want to escape the spider of rural boredom?

But the operation, although at first seeming a triumph, goes rapidly, horribly awry. A surgeon has to be called in to amputate Hippolyte's gangrenous leg. Charles is humiliated. As for Emma, Flaubert offers this chilling comment: she "did not share his humiliation, she was experiencing a humiliation of a different sort: that she had imagined such a man could be worth something." The operation, taking place as it does almost exactly halfway through the novel, is the keystone of the adventures of her soul. In the aftermath her efforts to escape her lovers are increasingly feeble. She starts borrowing money from Lheureux, the Iago-like merchant, and she starts begging Rodolphe to take her away:

> "But . . . ," said Rodolphe.
>> "What?"
>> "What about your daughter?"
>> She pondered for a few moments, then
> answered:
>> "We'll take her—it can't be helped."
>> "What a woman!" he said to himself as
> he watched her go away.

In one of his piercing juxtapositions, Flaubert shows Charles a few paragraphs later, coming home to gaze fondly at Berthe in her cradle and imagining her growing up pretty and accomplished.

The reader knows long before Emma does that Rodolphe will leave without her, and the suspense, as in most of the novel, comes from seeing not what will happen, but how. Rodolphe's farewell letter to Emma echoes Ernest's to Mazza written more than fifteen years before. Each invents reasons for his flight and moralizes in a high-minded way. "Fate is to blame, only fate!" Rodolphe writes. "'There's a word that always has a nice effect,' he said to himself." Indeed it does. Emma is ill for forty-three days after she reads his letter.

Flaubert is a master of two familiar devices that have a long history of engaging the reader: failure and repetition. Remember all those fairy stories in which the heroine must knock three times, or climb seven hills? Homais, who proposed the disastrous operation, now suggests that Charles take Madame to the opera in Rouen for the good of her health. And Emma, who refused to go riding with Rodolphe, refuses to go to the theater, only to have her objections, once again, overturned by Charles. When Charles goes to buy barley water in the interval and runs into Léon, their reunion has the force of the inevitable.

The return of Léon, rather than the introduction of a new lover, is another example of the skillful use of repetition. Alone together, at the beginning of part three, Léon and Emma talk. Their conversation, similar to the one they had when they met in part two, reveals how much each has changed. The innocent clerk has followed in Rodolphe's footsteps, becoming bolder and more manipulative. He claims to have made a will in which he requests that he be buried in the beautiful coverlet Emma gave him when he lived in Yonville. "They were both creating for themselves an ideal against which they were now adjusting their past lives. Besides, speech is a rolling press that always amplifies one's emotions."

But after Léon leaves, Emma, knowing the danger she is in, makes one last effort at escape. She writes a letter, explaining that they must never meet again, only to realize she has no address. She must deliver the letter in person at the place they have agreed to meet: the cathedral. This scene, part three's counterpart to the ball and the agricultural fair, is developed in vivid detail, first from Léon's point of view as he waits for her—"The church, like a vast boudoir, was arranging itself around her"—then, when she at last appears in a rustle of silk and thrusts the letter into his hands, from Emma's. In the Lady Chapel she prays for divine assistance. Briefly it appears in the form of a loquacious verger, who is eager to give them a tour of the cathedral, but Léon can brook no further delay. Fearing that his love will evaporate, he extricates them from the verger's speeches and summons a carriage.

We are not permitted to enter the carriage during that famous ride. Instead, we see the coachman's weariness—"Keep going!" Léon shouts whenever he tries to stop—and the townspeople "[w]ide-eyed in amazement at this thing so unheard of in the provinces, a carriage with drawn blinds that kept appearing and reappearing, sealed tighter than a tomb and tossed about like a ship at sea." We have one glimpse of Emma. Her hand appears beneath the blind to throw out some scraps of white paper, which at once scatter, like butterflies, on the wind. So much for her letter to Léon.

The white butterflies carry us back to the end of part one, when Emma, packing to leave Tostes, discovers her wedding bouquet in a drawer and throws it on the fire. The bouquet burns first quickly, then slowly, "and the shriveled paper petals, hovering along the fireback like black butterflies, at last flew away up the chimney." There is a risk to this kind of repeated imagery—that of the world seeming too well organized, sealed tighter than a tomb against the interruptions of life—but for the most part Flaubert avoids this by ensuring that each image is organic to the plot and to the setting.

The wedding bouquets, the damp walls and oozing trees, the cemetery and the pharmacy and the river
and the garden and the lathe of Binet the tax collector,
all help to bring *Madame Bovary* to life. How can we
question the actions of characters who inhabit such a
palpable world? When Bouilhet was urging Flaubert
to write the story of the Delamares, he also urged him
to set it in Normandy, the region he knew so well.
Happily, Flaubert heeded his advice, and the result is a
shimmering example of how much setting can accomplish for a work of fiction. The sharply specific details
of Tostes, Yonville, and Rouen enable him to get away
with flagrant coincidences, obvious foreshadowing,
and an occasional overuse of patterning.

How skillfully Flaubert depicts the withering of
Emma's hopes. In adultery, he writes, she has redis-
covered the platitudes of marriage. What could be
more distressing? And we, her readers, discover what
we should have known all along: that Emma's lovers
have only ever been a way of trying to find the life,
the intensity, she craves. She has indeed been on a
journey of the soul. In Léon's company she attends a
masked ball in Rouen. Afterward at supper she realizes
with dismay that all the other women are of the low-
est class. What a contrast to the glorious ball of part
one. "Everything," she thinks, "even she herself, was

unbearable. She wished she could escape like a bird, and grow young again somewhere far, far away, in the immaculate reaches of space."

When she arrives home the next afternoon a summons is waiting. Within twenty-four hours she must pay eight thousand francs. In a fashion eerily reminiscent of her fatal carriage ride with Léon, Emma dashes round and round, searching for the money. She goes to see Lheureux, the merchant, and finds him adamant even when she makes a pass. She calls on the bankers she knows. She begs Léon, who fobs her off by promising to approach a wealthy friend. She goes to see Monsieur Guillaumin, the notary, and rebuffs his pass. She even visits the tax collector. And all the time the knowledge that Charles will forgive her only makes her more furious—"even if he gave me a million it wouldn't be enough to make me forgive him for knowing me." At last she remembers Rodolphe and, as she had done in happier days, walks across the fields to his house. The conversation that follows, one of the longest in the novel, is by turns romantic, tender, mendacious, and furious, a model of desperate dialogue.

Just as the white butterflies of the letter carry us back to the black butterflies of the bouquet, so Emma's return to Yonville, as she runs back across the fields, returns us to that glittering night at the ball when, going down the stairs at the chateau, she resists the impulse to run. In the pharmacy she finds Justin, the assistant, who has loved her silently all along.

Question: Why does there have to be a Justin in the novel?

Answer: So that Emma can get into the locked room and eat arsenic.

The brutal elements of the novel, as Flaubert said, are everywhere.

Flaubert was a modern novelist not only because of his failures, his ambitions, and his self-consciousness, but also because he knew the value of research. He took notes at an agricultural fair, investigated the process of loans and debts, and planned Emma's wardrobe. Nowhere is his research more evident than in her prolonged death scene, the final adventure of her soul, a sequence unlike any that had previously appeared in fiction, one that many novelists would, I think, in its graphic physical details and relentless hopelessness, still hesitate to write.

The novel ends, as it begins, with Charles. He does forgive her everything: debt, infidelity, her neglect of him and Berthe. He even forgives Rodolphe and, in a moment of almost unbearable irony, offers him the excuse that Rodolphe offered Emma in his farewell letter: "Fate is to blame!" When I first read the novel, years ago, I mostly agreed with Rodolphe's assessment of

Charles: "comical even, and rather low." Now, Charles's love for Emma seems like a stream of pure and constant feeling running through the novel, "a river of milk," which survives every iniquity. Yes, I was right to think that he might, knowing everything, still have married her, but I was wrong to believe happiness ever lay within his grasp. He is, after all, a character in a novel by Flaubert. Another respect in which the great nineteenth-century writer is our contemporary is in his attitude to happiness. "It is strange," he wrote, "how I was born with little faith in happiness. At the earliest age I had a complete foretaste of life. It was like a nauseous kitchen odour leaking out through the transom."

In the miasma of that "odour" Flaubert wrote a novel that combines the vivid use of realism with the taut structure, repetitions, and reversals of a three-act drama. And because he never loses sympathy with either of his main characters, this union, unlike Charles and Emma's marriage, is almost wholly successful. Flaubert was an uneasy realist—he never forgot Le Poittevin's romanticism—but no one has made better use of the technique. When, years later, to please Georges Sand, he wrote "A Simple Heart," he borrowed a stuffed parrot to make sure he did justice to Loulou before finally turning him into the Holy Ghost. His precise details make possible extremity of action, thought, and emotion. As Emma and Rodolphe watch the fair from the window, and Rodolphe offers the romantic clichés that have proved so effective with other mistresses, an elderly servant is awarded a silver medal for fifty-four years of service on the same farm. Flaubert devotes a long paragraph to Catherine-Nicaise-Elisabeth Leroux as she approaches the platform. Here is his description of her hands: "Barn dust, caustic washing soda, and wool grease had so thoroughly encrusted, chafed, and hardened them that they seemed dirty even though they had been washed in clear water; and from the habit of serving, they remained half open, as though offering their own testimony to the great suffering they had endured."

HOW TO TELL A TRUE STORY

Mapping Our Narratives
onto the World

IN 1984 MY stepmother, Janey, died in the cottage hospital of a small Scottish town. I was teaching summer school at a university near Boston, and her death was, from my perspective, sudden. One morning on my way to class, I found a letter in the mailbox from an aunt. On the bus I read that Janey had had a fall and was in the hospital but not to worry, my aunt wrote; she was on the mend. I don't remember what I taught that day, but I do recall my anger. Her accident, I thought, would mean new problems, new difficulties, for me. I was still angry when the chairman came into my office with a message that Janey was very ill. I hurried home immediately and made arrangements to fly to Glasgow. Then I phoned the hospital only to discover she had died a few hours earlier. A week later a birthday card arrived. A nurse had written my address and a joke about my stepmother's many gentlemen visitors. Janey herself had signed the card, shakily, "love M."

I did not go to her funeral. I knew I would have to return later to deal with her possessions and I was too poor to make two transatlantic trips and too young to understand the complex reasons for which one might attend a funeral where no other mourner would be offended by one's absence. Instead I decided to write a story about her. The question was how?

Janey was almost sixty when she married my father and I knew only snatches about the large part of her life that had already occurred. I wanted to be faithful to her memory, faithful to the facts as I understood them, including our deep estrangement. And yet merely to transcribe the facts would have resulted in a skinny, parsimonious, undignified story. I needed imagination as well as memory.

Over the course of a difficult autumn I wrote "Learning by Heart." It was a long story, a hundred pages, with two braided narratives. One strand was based on what I remembered of my childhood and adolescence with my stepmother; I wrote that material as if I were writing an essay. Although I was presenting it as a story, I wanted readers to have that feeling: oh, yes, this really did happen. The other strand was my imagining of Janey's life, beginning in a croft in the northeast of Scotland and ending with those hours lying on the floor of her flat, waiting to be found. The life I did not know and had no means to discover, I dreamed up on the page. And in a number of ways I signaled to the reader that this part of the narrative had a different ontological status, was true in a different way. I wrote it as fiction.

I am not sure how well "Learning by Heart" succeeds, but since then, in and out of the classroom, I have pondered how the intuitive choices I made in writing the story might be refined. I began to notice that I often gave my students conflicting advice. A student would bring me a story about a family with three children. Sometimes I would say, "Why do you need Edwina, Margaret, and Theo? It just confuses your reader. Why not combine Edwina and Margaret into a single character and just have two children?" Sometimes, however, I found myself saying the opposite. "Why only have three children?" I would ask. "Why not have five? Or go for broke—have seven."

In the first case I was advising the student along the traditional lines of story writing: be expedient. Every sentence should, ideally, do three things: reveal the characters, advance the plot, and deepen the theme. The pleasure of this kind of narrative is not that we think we are reading about the real world (although the story usually does map onto our world fairly closely), but rather that the wings of symmetry are unfolding around us; briefly we are on a planet where, as E. M.

Forster says, there are no secrets and human behavior makes sense. I call this "fiction."

In the second case, where I was urging five children, or seven, I was suggesting an alternative strategy. The authority of the story was going to come, in part, from the degree to which it made the reader feel that the events described really had occurred. And the way to strengthen the story was to increase this effect. Rather than expediency, I urged the student to make the story messier, more confusing: in other words more lifelike. I call this, for want of a better term, "antifiction."

Throughout this century and the last, it seems to me, an increasing number of authors have been choosing to have five children rather than two. We can find story after story, novel after novel, in which the boundaries between author and character, real and imagined, are blurred. Our experience is closer to reading autobiography, or memoir, or history. I do not mean to suggest that there are simply two diametrically opposed choices. Rather I see a continuum, stretching from tales beginning "Once upon a time . . ." where we are blithely expected to believe that a wolf can pass for a grandmother, to the most explicit antifiction, works whose authors blatantly encourage what Sartre might have termed a hemorrhaging between fiction and reality. In Joan Didion's novel *Democracy* and Tim

O'Brien's *The Things They Carried*, characters share the names and occupations of their creators.

An Attempt at a Continuum

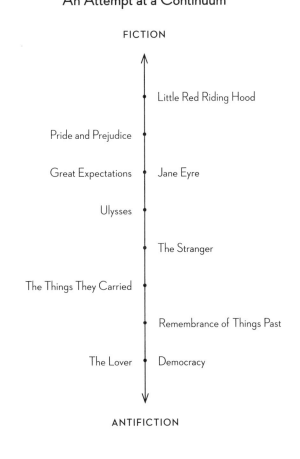

FICTION

Little Red Riding Hood

Pride and Prejudice

Great Expectations   Jane Eyre

Ulysses

The Stranger

The Things They Carried

Remembrance of Things Past

The Lover   Democracy

ANTIFICTION

Once I got a glimpse of the continuum, I wondered what lay behind these choices and how the signals are given to the reader. The first question invites a comet's tail of speculation. My suspicion is that most writers make these choices unconsciously, as I did, because of their prior relationship with the material. But at a deeper level, farther into the astral debris, lurks the question that we always need to ask: How can we give our work authority? By the end of her life my stepmother had very few visitors. What right had I to ask my readers to be among them? To endure the wallpaper and the antimacassars and, worst of all, her tyrannical conversation.

In a recent fit of homesickness I reread Robert Louis Stevenson's iconic novel of the double life: *The Strange Case of Dr. Jekyll and Mr. Hyde.* Stevenson claimed that he wrote a first draft in three feverish days, following a dream, and then burned it because of his wife's criticisms. Whatever the truth, the novel was written and published in less than three months, and I read it in a single sitting. Although it is set in London, the darkness and fog struck me once again as irredeemably Scottish. This time I was also struck by Stevenson's use of documents: Dr. Jekyll's correspondence and his "full statement of the case." Looking at other nineteenth-century novels—*Frankenstein, Wuthering Heights, Dracula, The*

Woman in White—I discovered a startling number of interlocking narrators, diaries found in locked boxes, deathbed confessions, and, of course, letters. These authors knew that their incredible tales needed authenticating and they approach their readers like a prosecutor addressing a jury, bombarding us with testimonials from expert witnesses.

In the twentieth century such devices fell somewhat out of fashion, but not, I think, because readers became more credulous (if anything our credulity has declined and we are liable to read a letter in fiction as yet more fiction). There are gorgeous counterexamples. Part of the brilliance of Nathanael West's short novel *Miss Lonelyhearts*, in which an advice columnist for a New York newspaper gradually succumbs to despair, is the inclusion of letters from Miss Lonelyhearts's constituents that are absolutely integral to the plot and to the anguished voice of the novel. More recently A. S. Byatt paid homage to the nineteenth century in her novel *Possession* by including fabricated poems. The novel captivated many readers but most, I suspect, soon realized they could follow the plot without reading the poems and turned those pages with increasing speed. Nowadays we find authors using e-mail, texts, memos, and blogs to shore up their work. We take pleasure in these devices but only in certain contexts. Broadly speaking we have decided to privilege memory over imagination. In the current climate a novel set in Afghanistan or Iraq written by someone who had never been to these war zones would be unlikely to meet with the rapturous reception of *The Red Badge of Courage*, which Stephen Crane wrote nearly thirty years after the Civil War entirely from research. Certain experiences—war, other races, some illnesses, perhaps other sexual orientations—are often deemed no longer appropriate territory for the imagination. We want the author to write out of memory. Even a kind of impersonal memory—the American-born Jewish author writing about the Holocaust—is preferable to none. Authors, along with other people, are now expected to have credentials.

Our confusion about the relationship between fiction and the real world is further revealed by our response to first-person narrators. Unless forcefully instructed otherwise we tend to assume that first-person narrators share the gender, and to some degree the history, of their authors. I still remember the shock of hearing that James Baldwin's mother had followed his coffin into St. John the Divine. But hadn't she died, I protested, conflating Baldwin's life with that of his narrator in "Sonny's Blues." In "Learning by Heart" I did not bother for many pages to identify the first-person narrator as a young woman, a version of myself; I knew the reader would think that anyway.

These assumptions, which can do so much for our work when we follow them, become more problematic if we want to contradict them, especially, I would suggest, for women writing about men. Ever since Daniel Defoe published *Moll Flanders*—"My True Name is so well known in the Records, or Registers at *Newgate*, and in the *Old-Baily*"—men have been writing confidently, in the first and close-third person, about women. A dozen great fictional heroines—Pamela, Moll, Molly Bloom, Emma Bovary, Anna Karenina, Isabel Archer—sidle out of my bookcase, swishing their skirts courtesy of their male authors. Relatively few men suited by a woman's pen follow. George Eliot writes with wonderful empathy about her male characters. And there is the male narrator of Willa Cather's *My Antonia* but he is largely overshadowed by his heroine's complicated life. Marguerite Yourcenar's magnificent *The Memoirs of Hadrian* was for many years almost as solitary as the great emperor. Only fairly recently have women felt able to inhabit their male characters, in both the third person and the first, as freely as Hanya Yanagihara does in her novel *A Little Life*.

Optimistically I like to think that this narrowing of the authorial authority has as one of its origins the widening of the canon, and the general recognition that minorities of all kinds are more than willing and able to speak for themselves. But I also wonder if it might not be linked to the surge of antifiction. Authors have been encouraging readers to map fiction onto the real world, and even when we want to, we may have trouble now in reversing that trend. Lewis Carroll's description in *Sylvie and Bruno Concluded* of the search for an accurate map serves as a cautionary tale. When a mile to a mile map is proposed, the farmers protest that it will block out the sun and ruin their crops.

❄

Putting aside these vexed matters of authority and autobiography, I want to explore in a little more detail what makes readers think, *just from reading*, that some stories really happened and that in others the question is irrelevant. As with the job interview, first impressions are vital, so let us look at the openings of a few familiar works.

Here is James Joyce embarking on the long voyage of *Ulysses*:

> Stately, plump Buck Mulligan came from the stairhead, bearing a bowl of lather on which a mirror and a razor lay crossed. A yellow dressing gown, ungirdled, was sustained gently behind him on the mild morning air. He held the bowl aloft and intoned:

Introibo ad altare Dei.

Halted, he peered down the dark wind-
ing stairs and called out coarsely:

Come up, Kinch! Come up, you fearful
Jesuit!

There is nothing in these events that renders them immediately fictional. In fact the quotidian subject matter could easily find a place in a contemporary essay, but Joyce gives us unmistakable signals that we are on the planet of fiction. Among these signals I would list the following:

1. There is no visible narrator.
2. The act of writing is concealed. We are made to believe that the words sprang up on the page without effort.
3. Characters are shown to us through action and dialogue.
4. There is no initial attempt at explanation.
5. There is considerable specificity of detail and a kind of heightened density to the style.
6. Both narrator and characters are unnaturally eloquent.

From our earliest listening and reading we have learned to understand these as the hallmarks of fiction. We are not allowed for one moment to take this as biography or history.

Here, on the other hand, is Proust at the beginning of *Swann's Way*:

> For a long time I used to go to bed early. Sometimes, when I had put out my candle, my eyes would close so quickly that I had not even time to say "I am going to sleep." And half an hour later the thought that it was time to go to sleep would awaken me; I would try to put away the book which, I imagined, was still in my hands, and to blow out the light; I had been thinking all the time, while I was asleep, of what I had just been reading, but my thoughts had run into a channel of their own, until I myself seemed actually to have become the subject of my book: a church, a quartet, the rivalry between François I and Charles V.

The paragraph continues to explore this confusion between waking and sleeping, book and self. In his dreamlike state the narrator ponders the act of writing:

"the subject of my book would separate itself from me, leaving me free to choose whether I would form part of it or no." There is an absence of dialogue and a lack of immediacy; right away we are being told that events are remembered. Most noteworthy of all, we are in the presence of a narrator who is not immediately distinguished from the author. Crucial to *Remembrance of Things Past* is the narrator's situation as an only child, and such is the autobiographical force of the writing that I think almost all readers are amazed to discover that Proust had a brother. Surely we can be forgiven our confusion when he not merely tolerates but encourages it. The narrator of this novel is not named for many hundreds of pages, but when at last he is, his name is Marcel.

Over and above these signals, a crucial and obvious difference between these two great openings is the difference between the third-person voice and the first. The third person is the "once upon a time" voice that signals we are being told a story. The narrator is not telling us about her own difficulties with a wolf but about those of Little Red Riding Hood. In "Learning by Heart" I was being absolutely conventional when I used the third person for the parts about Janey's life that I was largely inventing and the first person for the parts that I had experienced, or wanted the reader to believe that I had. But the way in which I used the first person would not have been possible without the example of Proust, and his many heirs. There were plenty of first-person novels prior to *Remembrance*, but reading, for example, *Tristram Shandy*, *The Red and the Black*, or even *Jane Eyre*, we have, I think, no impulse to confuse author and narrator.

Apart from anything else these authors carefully separate themselves from their narrators. Look at the opening paragraph of *Great Expectations*:

> My father's family name being Pirrip, and my Christian name Phillip, my infant tongue could make of both names nothing longer or more explicit than Pip. So I called myself Pip, and came to be called Pip.

Could Dickens have mentioned Pip's name a little more often? Reading on, we find in Pip's fanciful description of the tombstones of his relatives the density and unnatural specificity of fiction and, although events are clearly in the past, neither the act of remembering nor the act of writing is invoked. My first thought was that even a reader who knew nothing of Dickens's early life would suspect that more than the name of the narrator was being fictionalized. But that is the wrong way round. We are being so clearly signaled that this is fiction that the question "Did these things really happen?" does not occur to us any more than we ask if a prince could really climb up the rope of Rapunzel's hair. This kind of opening was later passionately subverted by Salinger's Holden Caulfield, who announces that he is not going to tell us "where I was born, and what my lousy childhood was like, and . . . all that David Copperfield kind of crap."

In shifting the boundaries between the self and the book, Proust, I would argue, has had a far greater influence than Joyce. A host of fictional memoirs (what the French call "autofiction") have been published since *Remembrance of Things Past*, some of which have sought to extend the continuum of antifiction even further. How far this can be done without the reader wondering why this material is being presented as fiction is a question to ponder. In 1984 the French writer Marguerite Duras, after a long silence, published a short novel, *The Lover*. The novel revolves around the relationship between a fifteen-and-a-half-year-old French girl and her twenty-seven-year-old Chinese lover. The American edition had a photograph of the young Duras on the front cover, and it was widely mentioned in reviews that the novel was largely, if not entirely, autobiographical.

Putting aside these marketing techniques, one of the most striking aspects of the opening pages of *The Lover* is the way in which Duras's first-person narrator, who seems to share everything with her author, shuttles back and forth between France and Indochina, between her present self and her fifteen-year-old self. This could, I suppose, give the effect of muddle or disorganization, but in fact it strengthens our sense that the events described are historical rather than imaginary. Duras is simply remembering, looking back over many years, and picking out what she wants to tell us. When I went back to "Learning by Heart" I discovered I had, unwittingly, used the same strategy. Janey's story, the story I was imagining, moved steadily forward with the occasional memory or flashback embedded in the flow; it was hard enough to make things up without making them up out of order. But in the part where I was combining memory and imagination, trying to smuggle in as much real-world material as possible, I found it hard to progress chronologically. Describing Janey's marriage to my father, I skipped a quarter of a century to report my reading of the letters she received at that time. As I read again and again the phrases of congratulation— *Your husband is a lucky man; We wish you much happiness*—I gradually understood that Janey had entirely failed to mention my existence.

In the nineteenth century Duras would probably have used letters, or a sensational secret diary, to support her story. Late in the twentieth century, however, she relied upon a heavy hemorrhaging between reality and fiction. No one could attack the plot because she was claiming that these events really happened, but if pressed too closely, she could protest that this was fiction; she had invented everything. Several times in *The Lover*, the narrator remarks that she has never written about this material before and, now that she is, she plans to tell the whole truth and nothing but the truth. Even fairly soon after publication astute critics were diagnosing a hole in the heart of the novel. And subsequently Duras agreed with them. In 1991 she published *The North China Lover*, which revealed what had been concealed by the scandalous affair in *The Lover*—namely her narrator's incestuous relationship with her younger brother.

I do not mean to sound as if I am taking Duras to task for mendacity. My concern is not whether the events described in a work of fiction occurred, but rather the techniques by which an author might make a reader believe that they can be mapped onto the real world. All authors—whether writing traditional fiction, antifiction, or nonfiction—omit and select. When I discover that Proust had a brother, it does not detract from the beauty and authenticity of his portrayal of an only child. In "Learning by Heart" I describe at length the loneliness of living with my father and stepmother. I do not mention the neighbors with whom I often took refuge and who would later become my beloved adopted family. I like to think that this omission is not merely a bid for reader sympathy but also a way to dramatize my relationship with Janey more clearly. No, my charge against Duras is not the omission, per se, but the way in which the omission sometimes flattens rather than dramatizes the novel.

Vagueness, the invocation of remembering and writing, shuttling, hemorrhaging, the absence of dialogue—all help to create the illusion of antifiction. Another strategy, one I seldom advocate to my students, is what I am rather nervously going to call "bad writing." Fiction tends to be well written. A surprising number of characters and narrators reach what, if we stop to think (but of course we don't), are quite unrealistic heights of eloquence. It follows then that one way for an author to make her or his work more lifelike is by the judicious use of bad writing.

I was a little hard-pressed to find an example of this outside of my own work, but you can glimpse what I'm suggesting in the opening of Albert Camus's novel *The Stranger*, a novel for which I have great admiration:

> Maman died today. Or yesterday maybe, I don't know. I got a telegram from the home: "Mother deceased. Funeral

tomorrow. Faithfully yours." That doesn't mean anything. Maybe it was yesterday.

The old people's home is at Marengo, about eighty kilometers from Algiers, I'll take the two o'clock bus and get there in the afternoon. That way I can be there for the vigil and come back tomorrow night. I asked my boss for two days off and there was no way he was going to refuse me with an excuse like that.

To seriously call this bad writing would be a woeful error, but the cunningly crafted sentences are flat almost to the point of being simplistic. Even though they demonstrate what Flaubert calls "fundamental accuracy of detail," many writers would hesitate to write them. They seem too unadorned, too unliterary, to transport the reader. But in *The Stranger* they effectively create a narrator in whose capacity for violence and lack of self-analysis we come to vividly believe. The antifictional quality is further strengthened by the uncertainty: "Maman died today. Or yesterday maybe." After all, if it's fiction, there is no reason for any uncertainty. We are making things up, so we can make them up precisely.

From these opening sentences Camus leads us forward to the moment when Meursault, the narrator, kills a man on the beach, a crime for which he offers no explanation and shows little remorse. Which leads us to another technique of antifiction. Motivation is one of the principle ways in which fiction makes sense. Terrible things may happen, indeed they often do, but we understand why. Readers are deeply committed to this aspect of fiction, and even when a writer tries to prevent them from making certain connections, they insist on doing so.

But one of the most frightening things about the world we inhabit is that action and motivation are not so neatly connected. Putting aside the complex issues that fill the newspapers, we often struggle to understand the behavior of family and friends, and yet even they, I would suggest, are more transparent to us than we are to ourselves. How easily we complete such sentences as "He's afraid of anger because . . ." or "She can't finish her novel because . . ." Yet how hard it can be to finish those sentences when we ourselves are the subject. Hours of conversation, therapy, walking the Appalachian Trail, may be necessary before we find an explanation that clarifies our own inner workings, and that explanation is often provisional, a work in progress. Part of what Camus accomplishes in *The Stranger* is the creation of a much more complex psychological model, a model that partakes not so much of the glibness with which we too often analyze others but of the sense of mystery with which we regard ourselves. We are our own terra incognita, the country on ancient maps where dragons lurk.

In writing about Janey, I felt reluctant—to the point of paralysis—to attribute motivation to her. She was a giant of my childhood and neither time nor mortality can dwarf her. I knew I couldn't offer my readers the pleasures of conventional fiction: explanations, those moments when cause and effect come together. So I had to give them another kind of satisfaction; I used the techniques of antifiction to suggest that the relationship between Janey and me, the fourteen years we lived together, really had occurred.

❀

Private history plays a part in most fiction but, public history is often in short supply. While there are admirable novels that deal with war, technology, politics, fracking, immigration, the Edict of Nantes, it is surprising how many works of fiction contain almost no references to current events. Jane Austen has often been taken to task for not mentioning the Battle of Waterloo (although only *Persuasion* was written after the battle). Since then many other writers have followed in her footsteps, focusing almost entirely on the characters and their relationships. *A Little Life* takes place over several decades but Yanagihara makes almost no reference to American politics. And in many other novels we learn surprisingly little about the real world: an odd newspaper headline, or a few phrases of radio news. Perhaps this suggests a mutual longing, shared by both writers and readers, for art to transcend the everyday. Perhaps it also stems from the danger of such references seeming expository, or becoming dated.

Whatever the source of this exclusion, it also means that as soon as we start to connect the lives of our characters with the real world, we are taking a step toward making our fiction sound like antifiction. From the ages of nine to thirteen I attended a girls' school that I prayed nightly would be destroyed: burned to the ground or flattened by a hurricane. I didn't care which. But in "Learning by Heart," I explained that when the school did finally close it was due neither to arson nor prayer but to the shrinking of the British colonies, which led to fewer people working abroad and sending their daughters home to be educated. (I had my revenge on the school when I renamed it, and made it several times more Dickensian, in my novel *The Flight of Gemma Hardy*.)

Here is a list of the techniques I've been suggesting.

FICTION	ANTIFICTION
Tidy (2 Kids)	Messy (5 Kids)
No Visible Narrator	Hemorrhaging
Act of Writing/ Remembering Concealed	Act of Writing/ Remembering Invoked
Action + Dialogue	Lack of Immediacy
Specificity/Density	Vagueness
Chronology: A > B > C	Skipping/Shuttling
Eloquence	"Bad" Writing
Post-Freudian Psychology	Lack of Causation
No History	History
Clarity	Confusion/Ambiguity
There Are No Accidents	Perhaps there are . . .

All these techniques (with the notable exception of bad writing) are used to gorgeous effect in Tim O'Brien's *The Things They Carried*. This book, dedicated to its characters, takes as one of its main themes the connection between fact and fiction. For the sake of simplicity I have been presenting my argument as if the techniques of fiction and antifiction were in opposition—one must choose entirely from either one column or the other—but O'Brien, and many of my favorite writers, demonstrate how they can be successfully combined. The stories in *The Things They Carried* range along the continuum from the highly fictional "Sweetheart of the Song Tra Bong," about a soldier smuggling his girlfriend into Vietnam, to the highly antifictional "How to Tell a True War Story." In the antifiction stories O'Brien offers us the specificity and eloquence of fiction but uses historical details, vagueness, and shuttling to reject an easy psychology of cause and effect. He often invokes the acts of remembering and of writing: "I'm forty-three years old, and a writer now, and even still, right here, I keep dreaming Linda alive."

In "How to Tell a True War Story" the narrator says if you ask whether the story is true and the answer matters, you've got your answer:

For example, we've all heard this one. Four guys go down a trail. A grenade sails out. One guy jumps on it and takes the blast and saves his three buddies.

Is it true?

The answer matters.

You'd feel cheated if it never happened. . . . Yet even if it did happen . . . you know it can't be true, because a true war story does not depend upon that kind of truth. Absolute occurrence is irrelevant. A thing may happen and be a total lie; another thing may not happen and be truer than the truth.

Here I think O'Brien delineates the dilemma of all serious fiction writers. However we approach our work and the world, we are trying to get at the truth that lies beyond absolute occurrence.

Most of the examples I've offered demonstrate the strength of antifiction—how using these techniques can enable us to tell stories that would otherwise strike the reader as too farfetched, too extreme—but one of the major hazards of the enterprise can be seen in an editor's response to a book of personal essays about Israel written by a friend of mine. "Very nice," she said, "but who would want to read about you?" I immediately applied this chilling question to myself. When I stop to think, it seems very odd that I would never want to write my autobiography—my life is so pedestrian—and yet I persisted in writing a story as autobiographical as "Learning by Heart."

The answer to this apparent contradiction lies in the nature of fiction, and of art in general. Art has the power to transform, and nowhere is that power more evident than when applied to the unpromising material of the everyday. *Madame Bovary*, with its sensational plot, made Gustave Flaubert famous, but his artistry is perhaps even more evident in the novella he wrote twenty years later. In "A Simple Heart" he transforms the relationship between a poorly educated serving woman and her parrot into a subject of resonance, beauty, and, finally, spiritual transcendence.

In the case of Janey, however, I lacked confidence in my ability to transform; there were too many suitcases of truth, too many things that I still didn't understand, that I wanted to smuggle into the story. I would never have gotten them all onto the planet of fiction. Instead I tried to create the illusion that Janey had lived and died in the way I described. I knew that this illusion could be immensely seductive, but that if I failed to rise above the anecdotal then the reader would balk and ask, Why should I want to read about Janey and you?

As a young writer, I made these choices intuitively, often not fully understanding what I was choosing. As an older writer, I've learned how useful these different techniques can be, how they can help me tell the stories I couldn't otherwise tell. In *The Prince* Machiavelli, the Florentine philosopher and diplomat, urges princes to become great liars. In the service of absolute truth writers need to follow his advice. We have stories we want to tell and many, happily, belong on the planet of fiction, where readers can delight in eloquent characters, precise narrators, and the pleasing symmetry of cause and effect. But some of the stories we want to tell may be too implausible, too contradictory, too psychologically outrageous to exist on that planet. Only by suggesting a different ontology, a different relationship to the real world, can we persuade readers to suspend their disbelief. So we head to the dark star of antifiction.

Will we send our work into the world as fiction? Antifiction? Or some cunning mixture of the two? As Proust's narrator so simply and elegantly says, "[T]he subject of my book would separate itself from me, leaving me free to choose whether I would form part of it or not." Whether we hide behind a third or first-person narrator very different from ourselves or, alternatively, we encourage our readers to confuse the cunningly created "I" of our stories with the I of our lives, we are always seeking authority for our work. The question is what the source will be.

SHAKESPEARE
FOR WRITERS

Learning from the Master

IT WOULD NOT be entirely accurate to claim that Shakespeare is a writer with whom I have a lifelong acquaintance, although perhaps my mother attended a production of *Twelfth Night* or *Hamlet* when I was in utero. And I like to think that she may have read aloud to me from Lamb's *Tales from Shakespeare*; as a nurse during the Second World War, she survived many months of night duty by reading novels. As for my father, at trying moments he frequently quoted King Lear's complaint: "How sharper than a serpent's tooth it is / To have a thankless child." My own independent relationship with Shakespeare began when I was nine, the year I started elocution lessons. These were held in the drawing room of the girls' private school I attended at that time. I remember lying on the carpeted floor, staring up at the walls, which were paneled in yellow fabric, and practicing breathing from the diaphragm.

Then I was allowed to stand up and recite Puck's speech from *A Midsummer Night's Dream*:

> Through the forest have I gone,
> But Athenian found I none,
> On whose eyes I might approve
> This flower's force in stirring love.

Later that year I was cast as Jessica, Shylock's daughter, in *The Merchant of Venice*. I gazed raptly at Lorenzo, played by another nine-year-old girl, while he declaimed:

> How sweet the moonlight sleeps upon
>   this bank.
> Here will we sit and let the sounds of music
> Creep in our ears; soft stillness and the night
> Become the touches of sweet harmony.
> Sit, Jessica. Look how the floor of heaven
> Is thick inlaid with patens of bright gold.
> There's not the smallest orb which thou
>   behold'st
> But in his motion like an angel sings,
> Still quiring to the young-eyed cherubins.
> Such harmony is in immortal souls,
> But whilst this muddy vesture of decay
> Doth grossly close it in, we cannot hear it.

And how did Jessica respond to these beautiful words? I regret to report she says only, "I am never merry when I hear sweet music." No wonder I envied my suitor and learned his lines as well as my own.

From then on I studied several plays a year. I was particularly enthralled by *Macbeth* with its Scottish setting. We often drove past Birnam Wood on our way to visit my aunt, and I always remembered the witches' promise to Macbeth—that he is safe until Birnam Wood comes to Dunsinane Hill—and how cleverly the meaning of that promise is subverted, by having the soldiers carry broken-off branches as camouflage. For a few years in the 1990s the town of Birnam offered something called "The Macbeth Experience." Sadly it closed before I had a chance to investigate.

In spite of this long acquaintance, however, I only recently began to consider what I could learn as a writer from our great forebear. The major plays, surrounded as they are by mountain ranges of criticism, seem at first glance too formidable to use as models, but when one surmounts, or in my own case largely ignores, those mountains, the texts prove to be a treasure trove of lustrous examples, useful precepts, helpful strategies, and magnificent language.

Although Shakespeare's life remains largely mysterious, and contributes only marginally to our understanding of his work, a few key facts are germane. Popular tradition has it that he was born on St. George's Day, April 23, 1564, and died on the same day in 1616. His mother was the daughter of a well-to-do landowner; his father a glove maker, tanner, and trader in wool. Some sources claim that his father also lent money at interest, which makes one reconsider the jibes hurled at Shylock. Shakespeare married Anne Hathaway in 1582, when he was eighteen and she was twenty-six; their first child, Susanna, was born six months later. The twins Hamnet and Judith followed in 1585. Little is known, though much is theorized, about how Shakespeare made his way from Stratford-upon-Avon to London and became first an actor, then a playwright and theater manager. In 1595 he is listed among the senior members of the Lord Chamberlain's Men and in 1598 he took a share in the new Globe playhouse. Throughout all this his family seems to have remained in Stratford. Like many of his characters, Shakespeare moved back and forth between two worlds: the urban bustle of London and the rural calm of a country town. He died in Stratford at the shockingly young age of fifty-two.

Whatever else he was doing during his life, Shakespeare wrote. Thirty-six plays are, more or less, attributed to him, along with several long poems and the beloved sonnets. Of the plays perhaps half are performed and read frequently. Looking at several of those that aren't was instructive. While there are wonderful moments, gorgeous turns of phrase, I also found him making poor use of two of his favorite devices: mistaken identity and/or disguise and the (potentially incredibly annoying) feigned death. In *Cymbeline* the heroine, Imogen, disguised as the page Fidele, awakes beside a headless corpse, which she mistakes for that of her husband, but which in fact belongs to the thuggish Cloten. It was reassuring to see that Shakespeare could be less than great, and that it sometimes took him several attempts to find the right form for the material. *A Winter's Tale*, written the year after *Cymbeline*, uses feigned death and disguise to much more satisfying effect. Similarly *Henry VI*, written in 1590 and, for good reasons, seldom performed, helped pave the way for *Henry IV*. (The history plays were not written chronologically.)

Considering Shakespeare's work as a whole also reminds us that almost all writers are drawn back, unconsciously, to their own essential, one might say primal, patterns. Young writers often feel that they can repeat themselves because no one is paying attention, but, if we want to keep going, we have to become increasingly vigilant about recognizing our core material and turning a deaf ear to those sirens that would lure us back onto the rocks of repetition.

To discover more particularly what I could learn from Shakespeare, I turned to four of his best-known plays. First, a comedy: *A Midsummer Night's Dream*, written in the winter of 1595. Second, a history play: *Henry IV, Part I*, probably written in 1596–7. Third, what I would call a "tragicomedy": *The Merchant of Venice*, which was performed in 1605. And lastly *King Lear*, which was first performed as a cheerful Christmas celebration on December 26, 1606.

To begin, let me offer a tediously brief description of each play. *A Midsummer Night's Dream* is often regarded as Shakespeare's first mature play and is certainly one of his best loved and most frequently performed. Although the play owes a debt to Ovid's *Metamorphoses*, which, with its captivating stories of violence and transformation, was an Elizabethan best-seller, it is one of the few plays in which Shakespeare seems to have largely invented the plot, and the result is both intricate and simple. Hermia wants to marry Lysander rather than her father's choice of Demetrius, who is the beloved of Hermia's best friend, Helena. The four well-nigh indistinguishable lovers flee the court of Theseus to hide in a forest near Athens, where they get caught up in the feud between the fairy king and queen, Oberon and Titania. So too does a group of Athenian workmen who are rehearsing their own play about the star-crossed lovers Pyramus and Thisbe. Magic ensues. Eventually the lovers emerge from the woods, successfully reunited.

Henry IV, Part I shows the young Prince Hal, the future Henry V, emerging from the pubs and brothels of London to become a worthy heir. Like *A Midsummer Night's Dream,* the play is set between two worlds: the world of drink and disorder, where the stout, witty, pragmatic Falstaff is king, and the world of political ambition and unrest, where Henry IV, Hal's father, is struggling to hold on to his power. The question of the play is, will the dissolute prince rise to these challenges and overcome the ambitious, accomplished, and—in the production I saw most recently—compellingly handsome Hotspur?

The Merchant of Venice, another much-beloved and much-performed play, is set in a European country that we have no reason to think either the author or his audience knew well. It involves romantic love, but in this case Shakespeare combines plots from at least two sources—the casket plot and the flesh-for-money plot—to a more solemn end. He would also surely have been aware of several recent plays with Jewish characters, including Christopher Marlowe's *The Jew of Malta.* The casket plot is driven by Bassanio, who, well born but poor, seeks the hand of the wealthy Portia. According to Portia's father's will she must marry the man who chooses the casket—gold, silver, or lead—that contains her portrait. The wrong choice means forswearing marriage. Bassanio's friend Antonio, a wealthy merchant whose fortune is presently bound up in various ships, agrees to finance his wooing by borrowing money from Shylock; he offers his own body, a pound of flesh, if he cannot pay his debt. Bassanio's courtship prospers, Antonio's ships flounder, and the two plots converge in one of our earliest courtroom dramas.

King Lear, like *Henry IV, Part I*, is set in England against a background of political unrest. The elderly king decides to divide his kingdom among his three daughters according to who claims to loves him best. When his youngest daughter, Cordelia, says she loves him according to her bond, he banishes her and sets up house with his two other daughters, Goneril and Regan. Meanwhile another father, the Duke of Gloucester, is also mistaken in his children, favoring the wicked Edmund over the good Edgar. Terrible consequences follow for both kingdom and fathers, as Goneril and Regan fight for political power and Edmund's affections.

Each of these four plays begins with a wonderful writerly lesson: don't waste time. Don't bother with prologues, don't hold back the good stuff—just plunge your readers (or viewers) into an interesting situation that must be resolved. This might seem so obvious as to be scarcely worth mentioning, but often contemporary fiction relies on some combination of voice and a secret (shadowy, barely hinted at) to hook the reader. In contrast Shakespeare's opening scenes are full of tension, and the tension derives not *just* from the language but also from the overt conflict. Hermia's father wants her to marry Demetrius and Hermia wants to marry Lysander. Henry IV is faced with rebellion, and his son is too busy partying with Falstaff to help. Bassanio, despite lack of funds and the risks of choosing the wrong casket, insists on courting Portia. Lear is determined to divide his kingdom according to his daughters' rhetoric, and Cordelia refuses to play the game.

Also striking—again, reading these openings in the context of contemporary fiction—is that they begin in the present. No casting forward to the death of the protagonist three months hence, no remembering the night the heroine came home a decade ago to find her mother burning her father's tap shoes. Shakespeare does not use flashbacks, and his characters, with a few notable exceptions, are more likely to philosophize than to remember. The interesting and dramatic openings are happening right now and propel us into the future, not the past. Who knows what the great dramatist would have made of Harold Pinter's play *Betrayal*, in which, from the opening scene, we go steadily backward in time? Or Charles Baxter's novel *First Light*, which uses

the same device? I am not arguing against this strategy—the arresting event followed by the leap backward,
or forward, in time—only suggesting that perhaps present action is undervalued.

Another lesson to be garnered from these openings has to do with plausibility. The poet Coleridge
complained that the beginning of *King Lear*—the king
dividing his kingdom between Goneril and Regan
and banishing Cordelia and his loyal servant Kent—is
grossly improbable. And one might say the same of the
very peculiar business arrangement between Antonio
and Shylock. How many of us going to borrow money
would consent to sign away a pound of flesh? And why
go to a moneylender one has frequently slighted and
undercut, as is the case with Antonio and Shylock?

In *A Midsummer Night's Dream* we must negotiate
our way past at least two unlikely events. First we have
to believe that Helena, on hearing about Hermia's proposed elopement, would, rather than rejoicing that her
rival is out of the picture, betray the plan to Demetrius
in the hope of winning his favor. And then there is the
quarrel between Oberon and Titania, a quarrel so severe
Titania tells us that the entire world is in disarray:

> The ox hath therefore stretched his yoke
>   in vain,

> The plowman lost his sweat, and the
>   green corn
> Hath rotted ere his youth attained a beard.
> The fold stands empty in the drowned field.

The moon is pale with anger, and the seasons themselves have changed their wonted livery. The ostensible cause of all this is a changeling boy. Titania claims she won't give him up because of her love for his dead mother. Oberon offers no explanation as to why he wants the boy—perhaps simply to annoy Titania? But these improbable events happen so early, are so much a given of the play, that we are not in a position to question them. And if we did, Titania's gorgeous speech of nearly forty lines, describing not the origins but the escalating effects of the quarrel, would surely dissuade us from such unprofitable speculations. Poetry conquers all.

However implausible Shakespeare is in his opening scenes, once he has established the rules of the world he's creating—and he almost always is creating a world markedly different from the one his audience left to enter the theater—he is usually at some pains to keep them. Though we may quibble, mildly, over the number of convenient letters, storms, and resurrections, we appreciate his ambition to keep faith with us.

And plausibility in art is not always devoutly to be wished for. Certain gestures, while not making actual sense, make poetic sense. In Caryl Churchill's play *Cloud 9* a group of famous women from several centuries sit down to dinner in a thoroughly satisfying way. In Michael Faber's novel *Under the Skin* we empathize with the main character, Isserley, for many pages before realizing that she is an alien. When one stops to think about it, it is very odd that Cordelia's devoted husband does not accompany her to England to help defeat her sisters' armies. But we don't stop to think, in part because the play is rushing headlong at this point, and in part because we recognize intuitively that Lear and Cordelia, who have been separated by their mutual stubbornness in act 1, must now meet alone, without encumbrances, to work out their tragic reconciliation.

Similarly, we tend not to question why Portia, with no legal experience, insists on disguising herself as a lawyer and going to argue Antonio's case against Shylock. Poetically it makes sense that she and Shylock must confront each other and that, to save her husband's friend, she will employ the same verbal cunning that her father used in constructing the casket test.

One of the dictums haunting the lives of fiction writers—maybe those of poets and dramatists too—is Hemingway's remark that the writer can leave out anything so long as he or she knows what it is. This claim, in its most sweeping form, is surely indefensible. Imagine *Mrs Dalloway* without the party, or *The Great Gatsby* without the car accident that kills Tom Buchanan's mistress. Of course this is not what Hemingway meant; he exaggerated in the interest of reminding us of the artifice of realism and the necessity of selection. One factor in Shakespeare's enduring greatness is undoubtedly his gift for omission. While he works hard to make his plots seaworthy—here's how Portia got to the courtroom; here's some exposition to show how Gloucester died (offstage so as not to detract from Lear and Cordelia's reunion)—he does omit a good deal. Typically he omits journeys, unless they make a difference. He omits first meetings and courtships. He often tells rather than shows bad behavior.

And frequently he omits the psychological explanations so beloved of contemporary writers. Ford Madox Ford urged novelists to first interest their readers, then explain. While Shakespeare does an admirable job of following the first half of this advice, he often, flagrantly, neglects the second. Production after production of *The Merchant of Venice* struggles to make sense of Antonio's melancholy and of his huge, and not sufficiently requited, affection for Bassanio. A current popular solution is to make Antonio gay, but for most of the play's history, audiences were happy to believe in profound asexual male friendship of a kind they recognized from the Greeks and from various Elizabethan romances. In *King Lear* we are given no insight into why Cordelia is so closemouthed.

Of course Shakespeare was writing for performance, and anyone who has had the good fortune to see several different productions of the same play knows the profound difference that actors, directors, and designers can make. What he so felicitously leaves out, they fill in, assisted by his readers and viewers. In *Aspects of the Novel* E. M. Forster famously claims that if you write "the king dies and then the queen dies" you don't have plot, but if you write "the queen dies because of grief," you do. I would argue that readers nowadays tend to be very good at supplying the "because." When two events are juxtaposed we almost invariably tend to link them. A writer may try to thwart that instinct—insisting that the heroine's dream about a black dog has no significance—but readers will invent meaning and motivation.

In the case of Shakespeare, even when he does explain, he often undercuts or complicates the explanation. In *King Lear*, Edmund argues that his bad behavior is due to his illegitimacy, but Lear's legitimate daughters behave equally badly. Shakespeare is determined not to allow us to choose either nature or nurture as the key to character. "In sooth," says Antonio at the beginning of *The Merchant of Venice*, "I know not why I am so sad."

Other explanations are frankly unconvincing from the start. When Prince Hal explains that he is carousing with Falstaff so that, as a prodigal son, he will shine more brightly when he returns to the fold, we are, I think, rightly skeptical. (Although several members of the current British Royal Family seem to have taken this speech to heart.)

I am not, for a moment, arguing against explanation. How much less moving, for example, Tim O'Brien's story "The Things They Carried" would be if we didn't discover that Lieutenant Jimmy Cross's fatal inattention is the result of his hopeless, romantic daydreams. But I think there is a useful reminder in Shakespeare about the limits of explanation. His characters are almost always—Aristotle would be pleased— in action, and those actions speak as loudly as explanations. Flannery O'Connor's story "Good Country People" ends with a Bible salesman stealing a young woman's wooden leg, an event O'Connor claimed she had no idea was going to happen until fifteen or twenty lines earlier. Her readers at once recognize the inexplicable rightness of this theft.

Perhaps omitting explanations came more naturally to Shakespeare because he already knew the plots of many of his plays. He had read them in the work of other playwrights or in such histories as Holinshed's *Chronicles*. Given his many skillful appropriations, it seems particularly fitting that his own work has been so widely borrowed. The novelist Iris Murdoch famously claimed to have taken all her plots from Shakespeare. And many other writers have reimagined, or extended, his work. (I discuss such borrowing more fully in "Neither a Borrower Nor a Lender Be.") For now let me mention three essential aspects of his modus operandi:

1. He didn't conceal his borrowing. A play called *King Leir* was published in 1605, and much of the material for his *King Lear* came from Holinshed.
2. He often combined material from several sources, as in *King Lear* and *The Merchant of Venice*.
3. He was not afraid to make changes in the borrowed material: in the most likely source for the casket plot, the woman is a widow.

Using a plot familiar from either history or another work changes the nature of suspense. Most of Shakespeare's audience would surely have known that

Prince Hal was going to come to his senses and lead England to victory; like us, we may surmise, they felt fairly confident that Antonio would not die under Shylock's knife. We often say we're in suspense when we don't know the outcome of events and are longing to find out. But another species of suspense, equally nail-biting, is generated when we know, more or less, what is going to happen and are longing to prevent it. After many readings of *King Lear*, I still keep hoping for Regan and Goneril to be shocked out of their terrible behavior.

Sometimes the outcome of events is signaled as much by form as by content. Even though *A Midsummer Night's Dream* opens with Hermia's father threatening to kill her if she doesn't marry Demetrius, we know we are watching a comedy, a world where bad behavior will be less than fatal and love will triumph. When I wrote *Criminals*, my novel about a banker who finds a baby at a bus station, I knew from the beginning that I wanted the climax to be a reenactment of the judgment of Solomon, with two mothers struggling over the baby. In the first draft of the novel the baby fell to the floor and died. Several readers pointed out that I had not sufficiently foreshadowed such a terrible event. In revision, I revived the baby; she now suffers only a broken wrist.

Another lesson to be learned from Shakespeare is how necessary and pleasurable a subplot can be; to tell one story we often need another. *Lear* would be a shadow of its present self if the actions of the king and his daughters were not mirrored in those of Gloucester and his sons. In the case of *The Merchant of Venice* the two plots—Shylock's hatred of Antonio and Bassanio's pursuit of Portia—exist in almost equal relation to each other, one advancing the other until they converge. A third plot, the elopement of Shylock's only daughter, plays a part in both. Over and over, Shakespeare demonstrates that a successful subplot is one that is interesting and compelling in its own right, resonates with the main plot appropriately, and intersects with it at just the right moments.

A good subplot also has the virtue of passing time in a way that permits major changes, both internal and external, to occur in the main plot. The scene between Lorenzo and Jessica (which I so enjoyed playing at the age of nine) allows Portia and her maid, Nerissa, to return from the courtroom to Belmont.

This gift for plotting goes hand in hand with another of Shakespeare's great strengths: his talent for what I might call "social characterization." Such were the economics of theater in his day that limiting his cast was not a consideration. Not for him the two hander, or even the four hander. Most of his plays have casts of over twenty, and many of them have at least eight substantial roles. This is a large number of characters to bring to life; in performance, designers and actors play a key role in helping to distinguish them: Lorenzo is the one in a blue tunic, Regan has spiky hair. But Shakespeare also helps us by showing each in his or her social niche; even his outsiders—Shylock, Edmund—are defined in relation to society. Too often fiction writers inadvertently make their characters quite unrealistically friendless and isolated. But as Portia says, "Nothing is good, I see, without respect." Characters come to life in relation to, and in contrast with, each other.

This social characterization also enables Shakespeare to let us know almost immediately whether a character is a major or minor figure. When in the second scene of *A Midsummer Night's Dream*, we meet the six rude mechanicals—Peter Quince, Nick Bottom, Francis Flute, Tom Snout, Snug, and Robin Starveling—we immediately understand from the way they're introduced that Bottom is the one we should pay attention to; he exuberantly offers to perform every part in the workmen's play. At the same time the comic tone makes clear that he is a minor character. Meanwhile Quince, Snout, Flute, Snug, and Starveling are introduced as a group. We are invited to appreciate the music of their names and their idiosyncrasies without worrying about their psyches.

In *King Lear* Edmund is unmistakably introduced as a major character. In act 1, scene 2, he has the stage to himself and harangues us in a twenty-two-line soliloquy that begins:

> Thou, Nature, art my goddess; to thy law
> My services are bound. Wherefore should I
> Stand in plague of custom, and permit
> The curiosity of nations to deprive me,
> For that I am some twelve or fourteen
>   moonshines
> Lag of a brother? Why bastard? Wherefore
>   base?

The speech culminates in his ringing declaration: "Now, gods, stand up for bastards!" We are never in doubt that Edmund is going to play a major part in both the plot and the theme of the play, and we also know at once his position in society. His character is further deepened by his relationships on the one hand with the vicious sisters, Goneril and Regan, in contrast to whom he seems almost kindly, and on the other with his brother, the virtuous Edgar. Edmund and

Edgar act as foils: the character of each throws that of the other into relief.

I fear I can no longer avoid talking about the most obvious and the most impossible lesson we can learn from Shakespeare: namely what can be accomplished by the magnificent, melodious, rigorous, energetic, boisterous, vivid, inventive use of language. Over and over at crucial moments, and also just in passing, the words fly off the page. Titania's forty-line speech, which I quoted from earlier, could be summarized in a single sentence—the natural world is thrown into disarray by her and Oberon's quarrel—but who would wish it a line shorter when the imagery is so playful and so deeply pleasurable?

In *Henry IV, Part I* Hotspur and his allies, the rebels, are poised to fight the king, but there is still time to turn back. Sir Richard Vernon arrives with the news that one of the king's allies, the Earl of Westmoreland, is approaching with seven thousand men. "No harm," says Hotspur. And the king, Vernon adds, is coming in person. "He shall be welcome too," says Hotspur. Then Hotspur asks for news of the nimble-footed, madcap Prince of Wales, and Vernon, who has previously shown not the least impulse toward poetry, answers:

> All furnish'd, all in arms;
> All plumed like estridges that with the wind
> Bated like eagles having lately bathed;
> Glittering in golden coats, like images;
> As full of spirit as the month of May,
> And gorgeous as the sun at midsummer;
> Wanton as youthful goats, wild as young
>   bulls.
> I saw young Harry, with his beaver on,
> His cuisses on his thighs, gallantly arm'd,
> Rise from the ground like feather'd Mercury,
> And vaulted with such ease into his seat,
> As if an angel dropp'd down from the clouds
> To turn and wind a fiery Pegasus
> And witch the world with noble horse-
>   manship.

"No more, no more," cries Hotspur.

At that moment everyone in the theater, in the audience, and on the stage, knows that Hotspur's enterprise is doomed. He and Harry are counterparts; they cannot both exist. They must meet, and one of them must die. And it is the music of the language, the gorgeous hyperbole, the cadences that signal this just as much as the content. Knowing the outcome only deepens the dread and anticipation with which I watch Hal and Hotspur make their way through the battle until, at last, they confront each other, sword in hand.

Many young writers are drawn to what is unkindly called "purple prose," and most find themselves pilloried for their efforts. This kind of lavish, ambitious writing is easy to fail at and easy to make fun of. Almost all my own early work was met with rejections, dozens and dozens of them, that began with the chilling phrase "The writing is beautiful, but . . ." The typical response to this barrage of criticism seems, sadly, not to continue reaching for more richly specific language, deeper metaphors, but to retreat into a flatter, less adorned style. For fiction writers there is no way round having to write some fairly serviceable sentences—"Nina had spent the night in the living-room," in Alice Munro, or "On the bus to Dublin they did not say much," in William Trevor—but that is no reason to give up on the excitement and the possibilities of language. The notion of a painter who doesn't care about paint is baffling, but many writers (I exclude the poets) aren't that interested in words. They are convinced that the value of their work lies in characterization, plot, and theme. But these four plays, and many others in Shakespeare's canon, have survived, in large measure, because of the language he gave his characters.

He sets a daunting standard, and perhaps I've made it even more daunting by quoting only verse; for those of us who don't naturally write in iambic pentameter, this gives him an unfair advantage. So let me add that he also uses prose to admirable, and sometimes surprisingly modern, effect. Here is Sir John Falstaff musing on the field of battle:

> Well, tis no matter; honour pricks me on. Yea, but how if honour prick me off when I come on? How then? Can honour set a leg? No. Or an arm? No. Or take away the grief of a wound? No. Honor hath no skill in surgery, then? No. What is honor? A word. What is that word honor? Air—a trim reckoning! Who hath it? he that died o' Wednesday. Doth he feel it? no. Doth he hear it? no. 'Tis sensible, then? Yea, to the dead. But will it not live with the living? no. Why? Detraction will not suffer it. Therefore I'll none of it. Honor is a mere scutcheon: and so ends my catechism.

Was Beckett thinking of these dark repetitions and mortal puns, I wonder, when he wrote *Waiting for Godot*? I do not mean to suggest we should all be aspiring to write Shakespearian prose. Shakespeare himself, if he were writing now, would surely continue to reinvent the possibilities of language (I imagine him listening appreciatively to all kinds of voices: rappers, politicians, comedians, gravediggers, dental hygienists, Tony Kushner's lush lyricism, Elena Ferrante's intimate frankness). But I do mean to suggest that whatever your voice as a writer, you should be paying more attention to it—amplifying and enriching the language, bringing new words and new metaphors into your vocabulary and into those of your characters.

So harken ye all, do not let the Bard's mastery daunt you. His plays are a treasury that we can visit over and over, ransack and purloin as often as we need, and yet the gold remains piled high, waiting for us to return. Here are sixteen golden sovereigns I've carried away from studying these four great plays:

1. Begin dramatically.
2. Don't keep back the good stuff.
3. Consider beginning in the present.
4. Negotiate your own standards of plausibility.
5. Once you've invented your rules, keep them.

6. Don't be dismayed or surprised if some pieces of work turn out to be rehearsals. It sometimes takes several attempts to find the right form for the material.

7. Be careful how you repeat yourself, and why.

8. Remember the power of appropriate omission. We don't need to take every journey with the characters, make every cup of coffee.

9. Don't overexplain.

10. Be sure that borrowing a plot, character, or situation doesn't seem like theft.

11. Know which kind of suspense your narrative depends on, and foreshadow accordingly.

12. Be aware that form and tone govern content.

13. Does your plot need a subplot, or two?

14. Develop your characters individually, and in society. Let the reader know who are the major characters and who are the minor.

15. Be ambitious with your language. Write better sentences.

16. Whatever you do, keep making
    rhymes, puns, clauses, phrases, meta-
    phors, sentences, paragraphs, sonnets,
    scenes, stories, plays, poems, novels . . .

Shakespeare may not believe in explanations but he is good at apologies. Here is one of his most famous, which I also learned when I was nine, lying on the floor of that yellow-paneled drawing room:

> If we shadows have offended,
> Think but this, and all is mended:
> That you have but slumbered here,
> While these visions did appear.
> And this weak and idle theme,
> No more yielding but a dream,
> Gentles, do not reprehend.
> If you pardon, we will mend.
> And as I am an honest Puck,
> If we have unearned luck,
> Now to 'scape the serpent's tongue,
> We will make amends ere long—
> Else the Puck a liar call.
> So good night unto you all.
> Give me your hands, if we be friends,
> And Robin shall restore amends.

HE LIKED CUSTARD

Navigating the Shoals of Research

THE NAME HELGAFELL means "holy mountain," but when the mountain comes into view it is barely three hundred meters high. The track leading to it follows the shore of a small lake fringed with rushes. Dozens of swans, all facing in the same direction, drift on the dark waters. At the far end, I park beside a fence. A narrow path zigzags up the hill through the long grass. Despite its size Helgafell is famous as the home of Gudrun, a heroine of the Icelandic sagas, and as a place where wishes are granted. I climb slowly, taking in the ever-expanding view, occasionally startling, and being startled by, a sheep. Then, quite suddenly, I am at the top, standing on a broad plateau littered with broken rocks as if a giant with a hammer had vented his rage. The wind that only ruffles the lake below here blows at full force. Ravens arc and circle on the currents. I am struck by the loneliness, and by the fact that no one knows where I am. I make my way to the ruins of a hut, which my guidebooks variously describe as having belonged to a shepherd, a hermit, or some early Christian saint. Standing in its shelter, I take photographs. The landscape is typical of what I've seen of Iceland so far: bleak moors, bleak lava fields, volcanoes, active and extinct. Looking toward the sea, I glimpse three kilometers away the fishing village of Stykkishólmur, birthplace of my heroine Gemma Hardy. I picture Gemma standing in just this place, hearing in the cry of the ravens the voice of her lost fiancé.

As a young writer, I didn't realize that doing research is one of the deep pleasures of writing fiction. My early stories suffered from a surfeit of imagination and a paucity of accurate detail. To my youthful ears the very word "research" suggested dusty books, indexes, and crabbed notes. If I had wanted to spend my days in the stacks of a library, I'd have stayed at university rather than becoming a waitress. Writing short stories, in which often all that was needed was a glimpse of a combustion engine or one brief fact about breeding dalmatians, allowed me to maintain this prejudice. I had heard, too often, the old admonition: write what you know. But I was slow to understand the obvious fact: research could help me to know more. Slower still to understand that research has its own dangerous siren song.

After some years of working on stories, I wrote a novel set in contemporary Edinburgh. My research for *Homework* consisted of walking the streets of the city, visiting the zoo, talking to friends. After it was finished and published, I decided to write a pair of novels based on the lives of my dead parents. The book about my mother, Eva Barbara Malcolm McEwen, who died when I was two and a half, would be largely imagined. I knew almost nothing about her, but I was fascinated by the stories people told about her relationship with the supernatural. Patients complained that the hospital wards where she worked as a nurse were visited by poltergeists who moved the furniture around. She had companions who were invisible to most other people.

The book about my father, John Kenneth Livesey, who died when I was twenty-two, was an even more inchoate undertaking. He was fifty when I was born and his early life, like that of my mother, was shrouded in mystery. But I had read wonderful biographies about people who had been dead for much longer than him. Someone knew what Sartre was wearing when he visited Delphi; someone knew what Katherine Mansfield said to Virginia Woolf at tea. Surely I could find out about my father's boyhood, and surely something in the stories I discovered would suggest a novel?

My father had been dead for a dozen years when I
decided to write about him, and for ten years before
that we had been estranged. He was disappointed in
me. That is the word I remember from his letters; he
carried them into the room where I did my homework
and set them on the edge of the table. I wish I had
kept them—there were only three or four—but I read
them hastily, at arm's length, and tore them up. I never spoke of them; neither did he. A small victory for
British reserve. I stayed up late doing my homework,
desperate to leave our remote farmhouse, to study, to
travel. I never outwardly disobeyed my parents but my
father felt—how could he not?—that I was bitterly at
odds with my stepmother, the woman he had married
a year and a half after Eva's death. He had long ago
chosen her over me, and he continued to do so at every
turn. Night after night when the three of us sat down
to supper, I ate quickly and spoke little.

During these difficult years, and for as long as I
can remember, my father had emphysema and smoked
heavily. His false teeth were yellow with nicotine, as
were the fingers of his right hand. His clothes, the two
suits he wore for teaching, were threadbare to the point
of embarrassment. Need I add that I was young and
had no mercy? His last letter to me, written shortly
before his fatal heart attack, once again described his

disappointment: I was wasting my degree; I did not seem to want either marriage or a career. Of course I didn't answer and a few days later left to stay with friends. The next time I saw him, he was in a coffin at Perth Crematorium.

I did not expect writing a novel about him to make me love my father, but I did hope to recover that part of him that had been largely eclipsed by my stepmother. (And I should say I now believe he was right to choose her; only she could give him the care and companionship he so sorely needed.) John Kenneth was born two years after the death of Queen Victoria and grew up in the Lake District, where his father was the first incumbent of Skelsmergh, a small rocky parish a few miles north of Kendal. His mother nicknamed him Toby. As a boy he went to the local school and climbed the hills looking for peregrine falcons, but at the age of fourteen he was sent away. A grateful parishioner, whose son had been killed in France, paid for him to attend Shrewsbury School in the west of England. (Shrewsbury is a public school in the tradition of Eton; its most famous pupil is the Elizabethan poet and courtier Sir Philip Sidney.) My father went on to Clare College, Cambridge, where he did a BA and played golf. After graduation, he taught in several of the boys' private prep schools that flourished in Britain at that time. In his early thirties he moved north to Scotland, where he spent most of the remainder of his teaching life at Trinity College, Glenalmond, a school founded by William Gladstone in 1847 and still, I'm happy to say, going strong. His colleagues, for mysterious reasons, called him Silas. His pupils called him Jackal for his initials, J. K. L.

My father seldom talked, and I seldom asked, about his early life, but the various all-male institutions he attended kept excellent records. I sent letters—this was before e-mail and the Internet—to Shrewsbury, to Clare College, and to my grandfather's church, asking anyone who remembered my father to get in touch. I received a heartening number of responses, and over the course of two years I met with many of the elderly letter writers. These meetings almost invariably involved a journey of several hours on the train from London to some small town. There I would ask directions or take a taxi to the home of the interviewee. Tea would be served. The weather and my journey would be discussed with a thoroughness worthy of a Jane Austen novel. Then I would turn on my tape recorder and ask eagerly about my father.

"You knew John Kenneth Livesey. Do you remember how you met? What your first impression of him was?"

I hoped for stories—detailed, vivid, scandalous—that would bring my young father to life.

"Well, I remember him," my interviewee would say.

"What did you do together?"

"He smoked. I remember he offered me a cigarette."

"Was he a rebel? Did he have a girlfriend?"

"Have you tried the shortbread? My daughter made it."

What I gradually learned was that these elderly men, who had kindly responded to my request for information, remembered my father—they could recognize him in photographs—but they did not remember anything about him. This was finally brought home to me when I went to talk to Godfrey Clapham, who had shared a study with him at Shrewsbury in 1916. By the time I met him, in the 1980s, Godfrey lived in a small flat in a leafy suburb of South London. I was struck, when he opened the door, by his beautiful long face and by his frailty. He seemed barely to exist inside his suit. We shook hands—his, despite the summer's day, was very cold—and he ushered me into a small sitting room before excusing himself to make tea. I sat poised with my notebook and tape recorder. This man had lived with my father for two years.

Godfrey returned carrying a tray, the teacups rattling. No wonder his handwriting was so shaky. He asked me to pour the tea and began to talk about the swallows nesting in the eaves of his house, and the local train service.

"So you shared a study with my father," I said.

"Yes. I dug out some photographs to show you."

He produced two large black-and-white photographs showing rows of boys in dark uniforms against a dark building. "So here I am," he said, pointing to a plump, awkward-looking boy.

"And is my father here?"

After some searching Godfrey pointed to a pretty, fair-haired boy standing at the end of a row, staring directly, unsmilingly, at the camera.

"So what was he like?" I said. "Was he studious? Did he play sports? Did you stay up late at night talking? Did he believe in God? Did you talk about the war and whether you'd fight when you were old enough?"

There was a long pause. Then Godfrey said one sentence about my father: "He liked custard."

While he described how awful the food at the school had been during the war, I wrote down the sentence. Like most of my interviewees, Godfrey went on to talk about what really interested him: himself, his memories, his life. And I, as I had with the other elderly men, asked questions and took notes. If I could not find out more about my father, I could at least learn about his peers— that generation who had the blessing and the burden of being too young in 1914, too old in 1939.

By this time I knew a good deal about the First World War. In order to understand my interviewees better, I had read widely in the library at the Imperial War Museum, and elsewhere. Although this was before Pat Barker published the *Regeneration Trilogy*, before Sebastian Faulks's *Birdsong* and Michael Morpurgo's *War Horse*, there were many nonfiction accounts of the savage waste and sad heroism of what used to be called the Great War. I devoured John Keegan's *The Face of Battle* and Martin Middlebrook's *The First Day on the Somme*.

He liked custard. It is not a lot to build a novel around, but in my dozens of interviews it was the most specific thing I learned about my father. The novel I hoped to write sank beneath hundreds of pages of notes. This was how soldiers trained, this was how the lines of command worked, this was the amount of the tea ration and the bread ration, this was what happened to the wounded if they were lucky, or if they weren't. I still know a good deal about the First World War. I am still eager to talk to octogenarians. But I was never able to turn all the wonderful details about life in the first three decades of the twentieth century into fiction. My father remained shadowy, my plot vestigial, the psychological arc sketchy.

As for the novel about my mother, that too had a perilous voyage. It began on a misty October morning in 1987 when my adopted father was driving me to Pitlochry station. "Did I ever tell you," Roger said, "that the most profound experience of the supernatural I ever had was in the company of your mother?"

"No," I said. "Tell me."

Roger, like my father, had taught at Trinity College, Glenalmond. Now he described how he had visited Eva to make a phone call. In 1950 she was, as the school nurse, one of the few people who had a telephone. Eva left him alone to make his call and, while he was on the phone, a brown-haired woman in a raincoat came into the room, nodded to him, crossed the room, and left by the door on the far side. A few minutes later, his call over, Roger asked my mother who her friend was. When he described the woman and what she'd done, Eva told him to try the door he had just seen her open.

"And do you know what?" Roger exclaimed. "It was nailed shut." He swerved to avoid a pheasant in the road.

On the train I wrote down the story in my notebook and resolved to write a novel about a woman who is accompanied by otherworldly companions. The title would be *Eva Moves the Furniture*. My difficulties with my mother's book had, I think, the opposite source from those with my father's. In the case of my father, I thought I could transform research into a novel. In the case of my mother, I thought the subject matter was so interesting—my dead mother! ghosts!—that it did not require research, or even a plot. Of course I hoped to learn more about Eva, but when I couldn't, when my letters went unanswered, or came back unopened, I didn't head to the library, even though she had worked in a London hospital for most of the Second World War. I had sworn off wars, and research. They didn't help me to write novels.

One evening on my way to teach at Emerson College in Boston, I saw a group of people standing beside a bus stop, holding up a poster of a baby. Between one step and the next I decided to write a novel about someone who finds a baby at a bus station. Should that person be like me? No, I thought a few steps later, they should be the opposite. Before I started class I wrote down, "Banker, baby, bus station." A few weeks later I had a residency at the MacDowell Colony with my friend Andrea Barrett. While she wrote her wonderful collection of stories *Ship Fever*, I worked on a novel I boldly titled *Criminals.* Trying to avoid some of the mistakes I had made in the most recent version of *Eva*, I decided that this novel would take place in a short period of time and have a vigorous plot. As I wrote, I kept a list of things I needed to learn more about:

> Insider trading
> Being a recent immigrant in a small
> > Scottish town

Living on the dole
Betting shops
Psychosis

When I left the colony three weeks later, I had, with Andrea's help, most of a first draft. I plunged happily into the necessary research without worrying about being either overwhelmed or distracted. I had learned a lesson. I no longer interviewed people or took copious notes in advance. Instead I wrote the novel as best I could; then I went looking for what I needed to know.

Criminals found an agent and then an editor. During the long wait for publication, nearly eighteen months, I turned back to *Eva*. I had another idea as to how I might make the novel work. I no longer remember what it was, but I do recall the moment six months later when I knew that this inspiration too had been a snare and a delusion. *Eva* still had, albeit it in a slightly different form, all the problems that had made agents and editors reject the previous version. I turned instead to writing a novel about a woman who loses three years of her memory and falls prey to the machinations of her former boyfriend.

In the case of *The Missing World* I soon discovered that I could not simply make a list of things to investigate and keep writing. Even to draft some of the scenes,

I needed certain facts, certain insights. But despite the lure of neurological textbooks and Oliver Sacks's case histories, I managed to remain focused on my four main characters and their very different relationships with memory. The bad boyfriend became a beekeeper, which led me to conversations with some of London's many beekeepers. Another character became a roofer. I learned the nuances of flashing, the advantages of artificial slates. The key difference between working on *The Missing World* and my earlier floundering efforts with John Kenneth and Eva was that now I had a destination. I didn't know every stage of the journey, but I knew where I was heading; anything that took me too far out of my way was probably a mistake. I drafted scenes as soon as I knew enough to write them; then I did whatever research was necessary to fill them in.

Shortly after *The Missing World* was published, I had the now-familiar thought that I knew how to fix *Eva Moves the Furniture*. I had given up hope of publishing the novel but I longed to finish it to my own satisfaction and recycle the seven drafts that cluttered my study. I was walking down the Charing Cross Road in London when I stopped at a secondhand bookshop. I probably looked at several other books, but all I remember is picking up the one with a dark red binding titled *Faces from the Fire*. When I opened it, I found an account of the legendary reconstructive surgeon Sir Archie McIndoe, who in the 1940s ran a burns unit outside London; he treated many of the pilots injured in the Battle of Britain. I bought the book for a pound and began reading it on the way home. The Second World War, I learned, was the cradle of reconstructive surgery in Britain, and McIndoe was a pioneer of new techniques for dealing with the terrible injuries of the Blitz. Some of his young patients remained, even after fifteen or twenty operations, unrecognizable to their mothers, but he and they counted it a triumph that they could go to the pub without people fainting at the sight of them. As I read the vivid account of his work, I thought I had found the perfect metaphor for the complicated relationship I imagined my mother had with her supernatural companions.

Faces from the Fire helped me to understand something about Eva that should have been obvious all along. Like every child born in Scotland in 1920, she was growing up to face the Second World War. She qualified as a nurse in 1940 or '41, then spent the next few years working in a London hospital. I hurried back to the wonderful library at the Imperial War Museum. Happily for my novel—I wanted to set it entirely in Scotland—I discovered that Glasgow too had been bombed. I read interviews with McIndoe's patients, autobiographies of nurses working in wartime hospitals, and accounts of the Jewish community in London and elsewhere. Britain was fighting Hitler but not, as far as most people were concerned, anti-Semitism. Research, now that I knew how to go about it, finally gave me the tools and materials I needed to finish my love song to my mother. When the eighth version was finally published (on September 11, 2001), the four words of the title were the only part of the original that survived the many drafts.

Nowadays I feel that if I didn't write novels, I would have to pretend to do so in order to justify the odd, haphazard exploration of the world that I call "research." How else could I rationalize visiting Iceland and the Orkney Islands, talking to roofers and neurologists, studying beekeeping and Asperger's syndrome? Of course computers and the Internet have made these explorations easier, but there remains no substitute for the living encounter, the way a woman's face changes as she tries to tell you what it's like to lose her memory. Or a man's as he describes how he took that inadvertent step into insider trading.

Mapping my evolving relationship with research has made me think, once again, about all the time and work I poured into those failed pages about my father. He was a beautiful, charming, witty young man whose life was vitally constrained by two wars, poor health, the lack of both money and ambition, and a dominating mother. But it was my vision of his life, and not the life itself, that failed. Now I wonder if, with the help of Google, I could have shaped the material into a novel. For the first time I typed his name—John Kenneth Livesey—into the search engine. Here is the first entry I found, at the website for British executions:

> John Kenneth Livesey
> Age: 23
> Sex: male
> Crime: murder
> Date of Execution: 17 Dec 1952
> Execution Place: Wandsworth
> Method: hanging
> Executioner: Albert Pierrepoint

A thrill ran through me. My father, my deeply respectable father, was connected with murder, if only in name. Here was something scandalous, something more exciting than custard. Perhaps the name wasn't mere coincidence. My father was an only child, but his father might have had a brother: I could try to find out. Who was murdered and why? And what about the elegantly named executioner? How had he chosen his profession, and did he have a second job? For five minutes, perhaps ten, I took feverish notes. Then a blue jay scolded in the tree outside my window; somewhere an old-fashioned phone rang; I remembered the novel I am currently trying to write, which has nothing to do with my father, nothing to do with murder in the 1950s. I closed the search. But I still have the notes.

Acknowledgments:

The Hidden Machinery owes a huge debt to my colleagues, students, fellow writers, readers, and friends. And also to Emerson College, the Iowa Writers' Workshop, the MFA Program for Writers at Warren Wilson College, the Bread Loaf Writers' Conference, and the Sewanee Writers' Conference. My gratitude to these stellar institutions, and those who run them, for giving me the occasion, and the space, to pursue my ideas about reading and writing. I am also grateful to the Radcliffe Institute for Advanced Study for a fellowship which gave me the opportunity to explore homage.

Most of these essays appeared in a slightly different form in various literary magazines and anthologies. I thank the editors of the *Harvard Review*, the *Cincinnati Review*, *Triquarterly Magazine*, *Writer's Chronicle*, *Curiosity's Cat*, *A Truth Universally Acknowledged: Essays on Jane Austen*, *The Eleventh Draft*, *The Writer's Notebook*, *The Best Writing on Writing*, and *Bringing The Devil to His Knees*.

I am deeply grateful to the inspired, and inspiring, late Katherine Minton for inviting me to participate in the Thalia Book Club at Symphony Space and to Jennifer Egan and Siri Hustvedt for our scintillating conversations about several of the novels I discuss in these pages.

Without Tony Perez there would be no book. I am grateful to him for giving *The Hidden Machinery* a home and for helping me, again and again, to shape my thoughts. My great gratitude to him, Meg Storey, Jakob Vala, Sabrina Wise, Nanci McCloskey, and all at Tin House for their generosity, their acuity, their patience, and their genius for making the back and forth of editing and publishing fun.

Thank you Gerry Bergstein for giving this book such a beautiful cover, and for illuminating discussions on homage.

Thank you Amanda Urban and Amelia Atlas for taking such good care of my work.

Merril Sylvester taught me to read *Percy, The Bad Chick*. Roger Sylvester taught me to read Shakespeare. Andrea Barrett has helped me, for more years than I care to count, to think about the connection between my own work and the books I love. These essays grow out of our ongoing conversation.

For me reading and friendship are happily intertwined. I am lucky to share my life and my library with Susan Brison, Eric Garnick, Kathleen Hill, and several other ardent readers. Thank you.

MARGOT LIVESEY is the author of the novels *Mercury*, *The Flight of Gemma Hardy*, *The House on Fortune Street*, *Banishing Verona*, *Eva Moves the Furniture*, *The Missing World*, *Criminals*, and *Homework* and the story collection *Learning by Heart*. Her work has appeared in the *New Yorker*, *Vogue*, and the *Atlantic*, and she is the recipient of grants from both the National Endowment for the Arts and the Guggenheim Foundation. Born in Scotland, Livesey currently lives in the Boston area and is a professor of fiction at the Iowa Writers' Workshop.